Human destiny lies on our meal plate.

This apparent absurdity becomes clearer if we take a fresh look at the familiar.

Focus will ultimately reveal a vital web.

Vegan ninja

a cookbook of confronting ecological proportions and personal meaning

Paul Maguire

忍者

First published in 2015 by Barrallier Books Pty Ltd,
trading as Echo Books.

Registered Office: 35-37 Gordon Avenue, West Geelong, Victoria 3220, Australia.

www.echobooks.com.au

Copyright © Paul Maguire.

National Library of Australia Cataloguing-in-Publication entry.

Author: Maguire, Paul, 1954- .

Title: Vegan ninja : a cookbook of confronting ecological proportions and personal meaning/ Paul Maguire.

ISBN: 9780994232342 (paperback)

Subjects: Vegan cooking. Veganism.

Dewey Number: 641.5636

Set in Garamond Premier Pro Display, 12/17 and Worstveld Sling.

Book and cover design by Peter Gamble, Ink Pot Graphic Design, Canberra, and Grace Maguire, Canberra.

www.echobooks.com.au

contents

contents
continued

part one
foundations

fear
(basic truth)

Without doubt fear is humanity's most potent driving force.

Always has been.

It's deep within every race and creed.

It's not a sudden attack on each breath we draw.

That's panic.

Fear is a little more subtle.

And it's not just dread of things such as death, disease or downright failure.

Fear can creep into every corner of our existence day or night, an indiscriminate intruder skulking on the rim of our conscious, blatantly prepared to pounce on the seemingly mundane.

Like the weight of expectation on youth.

Regret on the doormat of age as our senses grey.

Regardless of how sophisticated we are, when fear cuts, we bleed.

It knows how to slither and defy logic.

In affluent Australia, like all 'advanced' societies, fear of change creates a common undercurrent.

Yet conversely we crave it.

This paradoxical unease gnaws at our brand name possessions.

It outlines us.

和

We've been condensed under the tag 'consumers' and conned to accept the contradiction of progressive stability in a purchase or perish mentality.

And fear holds us there.

Rarely do we innately touch the earth's life-force rhythm or restfully bathe our spirit in its pristine bounty.

These are antiquities.

Our inner sense of calm has crudely been run down by peak-hour traffic.

At the base of our spontaneous being a churned feeling persists.

We've been divorced from nature.

Civilised.

As creatures of comfort and habit, what have we left to settle our stomachs, our minds and souls?

The treadmill turns and our fallback choice is more of the same, the well trodden path.

Perpetual motion rattles inside our head.

We always seem to be reaching.

Reaching for something.

Then, in the flicker of an eye, we can be reeling from self-induced perils.

Tormenting ourselves.

Love and faith are obvious fear and greed predators, but they have largely been neutered by commercialism that's plasticised, sugar-coated, and dressed 'reality' in lingerie to market everything from cars to cucumbers.

And the latest is so much better than what's come before.

Constant updates confront and our response is fight, flight or succumb.

The majority among us succumb.

Truly, life is basic.

Regardless of our realm, cause has an affect, there is always *yin* and *yang* embedded in time.

No-one is oblivious to life's pressures.

Just as seasons chase seasons, weeks flow from days and meals should follow meals.

Our essential routines dislike threat, and the inevitability of change creates fertile breeding ground for doubt.

Our senses can be overloaded to a point of physical and emotional exhaustion.

That's when we're carried on an anxious current, downstream.

Can't you see?

Fear cannot be eliminated, it's as attached to our being as conflict.

Though, certainly, both may be overcome.

Curbing our violence and passing peace to children is an intrinsic step.

和

admission
(why vegan?)

A confession is the only honest way to begin.

I am no cook.

I am vegan though.

Julie my wife is a cook, but not a vegan.

We both live in hope.

And that is what this little book rests on.

With growing public awareness of the interconnected nature of individual choices and global consequences I hope the practicalities of a no meat lifestyle can have increasing appeal for people of all persuasions.

The future of life on earth may well depend on it.

That's a big call, but hey, the times they are a changing.

Climate the world over, at least in modern days, has never changed faster or more catastrophically.

And despite the improbable link between our next meal and life itself on this planet, the food we rely on daily could, dramatically in fact, help turn around mankind's environmental crisis acceleration.

I'd like to assist, if possible.

As the novelty of insatiable materialism decays beside humanity's outrageous pile of consumer waste and ecological degradation, now is the time to clean up our mess.

和

And there's no better place to start than with what we eat.

In fact it's elementary.

It's a primary source of existence, of nurture in many ways, and pivotal to how everyone will approach today and every tomorrow.

Food, especially the abundance that's taken for granted in wealthy western civilisations, allows us to indulge our social, political, environmental and economic wants.

These wants, I believe, have long required a revamp.

No doubt it's more than a little egotistical, dare I say downright pompous, for an ordinary Australian country bloke like me to entertain playing a solid role in such a shake-up.

Yes, I'm merely an uncultivated leaf in a tiny tree, quivering in the vastness of eternity.

I've long been the only vegan in my village though, so what is there to lose?

Naught, yet there's so much to gain.

While my small everyday voice feels fairly settled in its everyday clothes, there is an unease of mind that's tickled by a desire to be soothed as the breeze of rushing years rustles by.

I realise that being vegan is considered weird, or even a bit 'Mahatma Gandhi', by a majority of mainstream people where I come from, but it appears that view is abating.

Although the shift of acceptance is more city-based than rural, the nucleus of transition is very perceivable, even here in the bush.

Hopefully people who still see veganism as some sort of extreme health kick for an austere minority may gain from the following words a better grasp of this way of life.

Recognise it as part of a broader landscape and see it's far more than a fad diet, as detractors may postulate.

That would be great.

That is the main reason these words have been gathered together.

A personal need has also worked its way into the light of day.

Although just a commoner, I have a craving to publicly plumb the depths of the vegan concept.

If I don't have a say, others will continue to define the boundaries of my world.

And I've for too long been uncomfortable with such limits.

For instance, I think being vegan could rightly be described as an emerging universal religion.

It is where, for me, the practical, spiritual and philosophical meet.

I want to air my tuppence worth on that thought.

But unlike people who come across as if they know all about life, I know I don't.

和

So what this working class man lays before you now is an interpretation of what has been laid over the years before him.

At times I struggle for the right words. I know I don't need fancy ones, just the heart's truth.

And that is not always easy to touch, or convey, particularly when face to face with others.

I do not claim my thoughts to be original.

They really are a compilation of converging influences from various sources.

They're a collage.

My vegan notions are like fibre strands being wound together to form a sort of rudimentary rope bridge of understanding.

To be frank, each strand is a simple expression of my limited worldly experience and the bridge they form is as much for me to sway upon as anyone else, as in many ways none of us walk either unaided or alone.

We all move on occasions among unseen metamorphic surroundings, amid men, women, children, plants and animals whose influence we have but the lightest perception.

Yet those brushes with life-altering circumstance filter through our being.

Also, through the years I've been stunned by the number of people who knew so little about being vegan.

At times it has felt like existing as a member of a secret sect.

Like a ninja.

More than under suspicion.

A known provocateur.

Fanatical.

Shadowy, shrewd, outside tamed convention and, of course, threatening.

I stood beyond the pale of civilised expectations, somehow too wild and uncontrollable for other's traditional general comfort.

Admittedly, for ages I've secretly struggled with spiritual, humanitarian and environmental ethics and desired to infiltrate mankind's thinking and actions.

Like a ninja, I've been threatened and forced to fight off prejudice.

To repel the onslaught my arsenal, unfortunately, has been bolstered by righteous indignation.

The temptation has arisen to flash a star-knife at critical and accusing infidels.

Though, my weapons should probably be carrot daggers, rock hard potatoes or frisbee slices of beetroot.

What fantasy.

~~

At times I lose sight of the fact that non-violence is not weakness, it's where real effort and discipline lie.

和

Perhaps it would be better to sit down in a corner with the unaware and whisper: 'Pssst, listen mate, vegans are fairly common folk.

'Sure, we confront established thought because we don't eat animals, but does that make us some kind of subversive ninja cult?

'Possibly, because some people take exception to this challenge, but on the positive side of the argument we try to be ecologically aware, abide simply and try not to abuse life of any kind, including the human kind.'

I would emphasise the word 'try'.

In the main, I think everyone makes an attempt to be true to themselves and coexist in as uncomplicated a way as possible with all on our island planet.

But every path has puddles.

Vegans make a variety of ecological and humane lifestyle choices, some are obviously fruitful, some are less so.

We all make choices, from meat eaters to internet bloggers, atheists and Callithumpians.

We all have to deal with our own particular realities.

And they differ moment to moment, person to person.

Compromise is more real to most people than any purity of purpose.

And that's so for vegans.

We're part of a complex earthly mix.

Sure, being vegan is a commitment, but vegans are not perfect.

Stumbling is a regular universal experience.

Trust me though, a commitment sets our direction in far more ways than are understood at the start.

And if I can make one, and stick to it, anyone can.

Sometimes it's difficult, sometimes a snack.

Overall, I know being vegan can be easy.

And I don't just mean—go marry a good cook.

Although it helps.

Lots.

That said, the vegan way makes enormous sense in our household, despite two fundamental things.

Outside me, the other members of our extended family eat meat, many on more than infrequent occasions.

And secondly, when it comes to cooking I'm a jolly lazy sod.

I'd rather be out in a paddock doing something rural.

I prefer to picture myself as a basic gardener, an amateur tree gardener of sorts.

Cooking I see as hard work.

Creative, stress-free cooking that is.

Yes, I have a go and have tasted some domestic success, but the truth is that cooking time doesn't slip by for me as smoothly as outdoor pottering time.

和

Julie has always run the culinary side of our partnership, and run it well.

I've attempted to busy myself in other ways and Julie has pandered to my whims, aided and abetted my vegan bias, sought to accept my shortcomings and forgiven the times I've been cranked up over some confronting matter.

She has had her moments too, of course.

Then I've tried to steady the storm.

We don't always get the relationship right, in fact we have to continually work at it, but all up we've had a blessed existence together over more than three decades. So far.

A cook and a sneaky vegan.

We seek to best apply the ingredients of our now well-worn lives.

Everyone aims for that elusive balance.

And as we floundered along in our particular way it has become strangely apparent to me that a basic cookbook could assist everyone's search for equilibrium.

The world badly needs a cookbook on life, a vegan ninja cookbook, I thought.

So, here goes.

It won't be completely conventional.

Coming from a non-cook, how could it be?

While conventional cookbooks provide a straightforward guide for the preparation of food, I believe they only scratch the surface of possibilities.

I hope to scratch the surface of moral cooking, and stimulate thought buds about worthwhile existence along the way.

In addition to gathering together a range of quick, simple and more complicated dishes, this modest volume aims to arouse what lies behind our eating choices.

Why we humans eat what we eat, and the range of implications of our selections, can be more engaging than masticating over the actual items we put in our mouths.

The cornerstones of life also require some excavation.

Why would you become vegan?

How could you possibly live without meat, dairy products, honey or eggs?

('I just love the taste of steak ... of ice cream ... of cheese ... couldn't live without it,' people repeatedly say.)

How do we overcome the 'fact' that being vegan is radical and such a diversion from mainstream norm that it's 'all too hard' for many wealthy westerners to seriously consider?

That's like asking, 'what's the cure for thoughtlessness?'

Initially, we have to realise that there are genuine alternatives to a life centred on meat and animal products.

The options work well, are within most people's reach and can release any of us from our daily drudgery.

That's personally, without even considering global implications.

Veganism is not some bleak house in which the occupants deprive themselves of joy and apply superhuman willpower to endure a life of do-gooder's sacrifice.

~~

Once I made the vegan decision, I no longer had to pester myself about what I should be eating, or should be doing.

In the main, a sense of calm overcame me.

I felt I could see more clearly.

Physical, emotional and mental aspects of my life were noticeably nurturing each other.

Consumerism distracted me less and I became more able to concentrate on living each moment to the full.

In a funny way there now seems to be more options, not fewer, because my attention is drawn to what ultimately matters.

Abundance lies in simplicity.

And freedom springs from hope.

The bearing of my decisions shines brighter on the welfare of all life and our environmental impacts than on being 'cool' before today's consumer altar.

That's not to say I'm never dazzled by High Street neons, obliged to do what 'I should' or comply with other people's anticipations.

I'm as human as the next bloke and many is the day I still falter with the folly of perfection, trying to decipher what has to be done, what I'd like done and what can be done.

Actually, that's more like everyday.

Being vegan though relaxed the drag of commercialism, not completely decoupled me.

It strengthened my connection with duty to family, community, animals and our environment generally.

A sense of purpose and duty became enmeshed.

None of us though need have an 'all or nothing' approach.

Truthfully, that kind of thinking seems to doom most of us to failure.

Real goals are approachable.

And a dash of humility, optimism and fun to go with them can be great condiments.

Food is much more than just the tucker we consume to keep our physical bodies ticking along.

It is inherent in nourishing our spirit, and although it may be uncomfortable for many people to accept, the pollution, waste and resources used in its production and dissemination really do have vital outcomes for the sustenance of the earth on which we all depend.

和

Food is the most obvious part of being vegan and while it's an inseparable aspect, food is but a single element among many that comprise veganism.

Vegan food opens a door then assists in holding it ajar.

It allows us to see what being vegan is built on.

By itself though, vegan food won't guarantee anything.

Good health, for example, can be as illusory as luck.

Life is always unpredictable and vegans are not immune to illness, just as meat eaters are not assured of it.

But our chances of ailment and cancers increase with the consumption of animal fats, junk food, super sweet drinks and alcohol, smoking cigarettes, taking drugs, and simply being slothful.

Grotesque is a strong word, though probably appropriate when applied to the consequences of some of our species' ill-advised addictions.

Conversely, being vegan reduces risks and so improves our probability of better health.

That is exactly what it does for our planet too.

Life is about juggling options, whether we're discussing individual topics such as dietary guidelines, wealthy societies overconsumption generally, humanity's resource use or specific global climate solutions.

Being vegan can look difficult from a distance but the gap between mainstream 'normal' and what a vegan considers 'normal' closes markedly once we see that the mental hurdle to moving in this direction is more 'real' than any actual physical or technical barrier.

Consider the possibilities.

Even if you feel like a wooden peg among today's shiny polycarbonate ones, that's okay.

Loosen your mind.

It's worth the effort.

Adjust rather than attempt to purge the entire past.

You couldn't anyway.

Some old ways can hold tight—sort of like my dread of kitchen duties.

Well, dread isn't the right description.

I usually don't spend time in the kitchen under suffocating disease, it's more a feeling of incompetence.

Yes, I shrink from the cook's hat when I can, but I know the kitchen is our home's heart and soul in so many ways.

It's just not my natural habitat, particularly when an important meal is being prepared or time is short.

Sure, I can chop and dice vegetables, mix a bit of a salad, wash spuds, comply with recipe directions, fry, boil and steam things, but I'm more the follower than the followed in any kitchen.

I appreciate a lovely meal and the love that goes into

和

it, though when left to my own culinary devices, plain and easy defeats refinement.

An eye for simplicity is a ninja trait, along with knowing how to travel light and when to conveniently vanish.

Julie has said regularly that I've been of most assistance by mercifully not getting under her feet. I agree and think it delightful that people can at the same time be so similar yet so different.

Usually we're wind and water.

And, like any typical couple, sometimes we're earth and fire.

The fabric of our existence is ever being woven, creating a curious garment to encircle us, to debate and rejoice in as we flutter in the face of a shifting wind.

How often have the world's problems, great and small, been dissected while preparing a meal, around the table eating or when cleaning up afterwards?

Through open discussions we become more tolerant.

We strive, hesitate and slowly adjust our compasses.

We glimpse how little we actually know and how entwined we are with all forms of life.

And our footing gradually becomes steadier.

The weathering years act on each of us like osmosis.

Personal change can commonly drift on a random whim, but it's so much more meaningful if it's subjected to a little forethought.

Reverence grows.

Reverence for age, for those who have endured, with humility, what life has thrown at them.

What we distil from our worldly discourse continually seeps through our consciousness to help clarify who we presently are and where we're headed.

Refreshing our awareness helps balance right and wrong, heals hurts, incites humility and cooperation, triggers a need for action and provides relief through humour.

Humour.

Was it a taste for the comical that put the thought 'write a little cookbook' into the mind of a kitchen klutz like me?

Perhaps.

But I believe it was also a stroke of irony I felt one evening as a rowdy herd (some friends and part of the extended family) filled our Elderslie kitchen.

As we bumped into each other while chopping, dicing, washing and kneading we questioned a media news report someone had heard.

That interaction had tentacles.

和

rising tide
(issues)

Rising sea levels are making the island nation of Kiribati (pronounced Kirr-i-bus) uninhabitable and all who live there face having to move, the radio news item said.

It sparked robust debate among the six of us preparing pizzas at home together.

Kiribati comprises 33 atolls dispersed over three million square kilometres of the Pacific Ocean.

Most of its 100,000 people at the time of the news were crowded onto the main atoll, Tarawa, just above encroaching salty waters.

Environmentalists have predicted for decades that mankind's gaseous pollutants were accelerating global warming and contributing to the rising tide through ice meltdown and thermal expansion of oceans as the water heated up.

The warnings supported the view that the effect of rising sea levels would weigh heaviest on some of the world's poorest people who made a negligible contribution to the problem and were least able to adapt or take major steps to reverse it.

Kiribati President Anote Tong said the calamity of climate change had been afflicting his people for several years. Less rainfall, higher tides, destroyed crops, diminishing fresh water supplies, the bleaching of coral reefs that

和

cradled Kiribati, and increased coastal flooding had forced some villagers to higher ground and the population as a whole to seek the international community's help with relocation, Mr Tong said.

Back in our kitchen, discussion ebbed and flowed, like this:

'Scientists still argue the degree to which seas are rising, and the exact cause of it, don't they?'

'Some do.'

'Well, the situation's not conclusive, and what responsibility does Australia have for Kiribati anyway?'

'We're among the world's wealthiest and most wasteful societies, inevitably we should be accountable for our impacts and apply some precautionary principles even if there's a degree of doubt over the exact impacts.'

'Yeah, but Australians aren't completely responsible for accelerating climate change, major volume polluters like America are more to blame.'

'Right, but ...'

'Well, let America do something about it.'

'And Australia?'

'The government, and big business, could throw in a few dollars I suppose, as long as the other polluters do their bit.'

'What about us, as individuals luxuriating in the lucky country down under, what could we do?

No, a more appropriate question is, what should' we all do to reduce pollution and slow the earth's climate changing process?

'You know we could make a difference by cutting our coal-fired electricity use, parking the car more often and riding a bike, reducing consumerism's waste, recycle more ... .'

Blah, blah, and more blah.

The conversation faded, as if a volume switch was turned down in my head.

Words became hollow bells echoing in the cobwebbed vault of a weathered sandstone church.

Nothing more than platitudes.

How often does environmental examination peter out to a predictable pitter-patter, I thought.

Why does it reach to the core of a few people while gently flowing over so many others?

I looked down at my hands.

Kitchen voices softly pealed around me.

Vegetables I attempted to slice into edible order on the bench were vivid colours in my grasp.

I knew they held, at least, part of the answer to our agonising.

Society's burgeoning cravings for a meat-based diet contributed to the rising tide more than most people realised, I thought.

Yet the impacts of our daily meat eating seem to consistently escape proper widespread scrutiny.

和

Just look at the tree clearing for stock feed paddocks and land to run cattle and other poor 'edible' beasts.

Then there's methane from millions upon millions of their farts and burps and all the carbon dioxide from the meat industry's massive freight and refrigeration requirements.

You could almost hear my mind grinding away like a pepper mill as it crunched statistics to regurgitate.

The livestock industry, along with coal-fired electricity generation and humanity's petroleum-propelled transport pollution, comprise the three most significant factors behind the earth's worst environmental problems.

It is far from just Kiribati residents who should be genuinely eyeing the rising tide threat, I thought.

Eminent bodies such as the Intergovernmental Panel on Climate Change and American Meteorological Society, to name just two, have over several years compiled extensive reports on our warming planet, chaotic climate and rising sea levels.

Either you believe them, or you don't, so I'll pick just one snippet associated with one—the intergovernmental panel's major update which was made public in Japan in March, 2014.

On its release the head author, professor Ove Hoegh-Guldberg, said: 'Over half of the (Australian) Great Barrier Reef has disappeared in the last 27 years from ocean acidification due to carbon emissions, causing mass bleaching and death to many if its ecosystems.'

The reef now faced 'irreparable damage' within 25 years, the report said.

If global projections eventuate, other Pacific nations such as Vanuatu, Tuvalu, the Marshall Islands and parts of Papua New Guinea will also be among the first to go under the rising sea. Parts of India, China, Vietnam and Bangladesh could as well.

About 70 kilometres from my comfortable Aussie home, swathes of Lake Macquarie may even disappear below the Pacific Ocean edge in my lifetime.

Lake Macquarie is an urban sprawl city which merges into the outer suburbs of Newcastle where one of the world's biggest coal export shipping ports operates.

A record 154 million tonnes of coal was exported through the port of Newcastle in the 2013/14 year alone.

Alarmingly also, a study made public in February 2015 showed carbon pollution from Australia's electricity generation remained as high as ever, despite electricity demand steadily declining during the previous five years.

和

Burning coal, and an increasing amount of high-polluting brown coal, produced about 75 percent of our country's electricity.

An Australian federal government climate change study has found the Lake Macquarie area to be the most vulnerable site to rising seas and increased storm tides in our state, New South Wales.

About 18,000 hectares of land in and around the district are forecast to be affected.

~~

This sort of clamour between my ears continued roaring.

It jumped back and forth from my part of the world to the global stage.

With more than 70 per cent of the human population living on coastal plains and 11 of the world's biggest 15 cities on estuaries or coastlines, our entire civilisation should be seriously and urgently acting as one to address the issue, I thought.

Climate impacts are not just about the poor on Kiribati or a few rich people at Lake Macquarie getting saltwater in their private swimming pools.

You name it, extreme weather from droughts to typhoon-driven rains are deadly everywhere, my inner voice rehearsed.

And then—bang.

Urgency froze.

My incessant internal chatter faded right out.

Silence was palatable.

There I was, yet somehow physically detached from the scene.

It was peculiar standing in the kitchen, sort of invisible as I watched proceedings.

An indescribable sense of my own presence took hold.

Time began shuffling before my eyes, like arthritis.

It had ushered in this expectant, encircling quiet.

I could sense myself deeply drawing breath.

In and out, in and out … .

All about me had lapsed into slow motion.

I could feel myself standing at the edge of the room.

Standing completely still.

Observing, rather than part of what was going on anymore.

A couple of vegetables clung to my hands.

Less than two metres away a chopping board was in vigorous use.

It drew my wholehearted attention.

My mind was on animals being cut to pieces, becoming bloody blobs of 'meat'.

It was like peering into a nightmare.

Blood ran along the knife blade.

A little of it trickled down fingers and dripped onto the board.

The sound of steel cutting onto the wood ricocheted off my conscious.

No-one else noticed.

和

The outside world was wafting around our home.

It was so casual I could almost caress it.

Everyone else in the kitchen was too busy.

Yet I was uncomfortable, sort of prying on something not meant to be seen.

Animal pieces were being sliced, sliced into smaller and smaller portions.

Before my eyes the tiniest of tiny pieces and blood seemed to be turning into a thin haunting steam and then floating out the window.

As the steam came in contact with the outside world everything was gradually enveloped in the mist of dusk.

Backyard trees were dimming and disappearing from view in this spreading mist.

The aerosol atmosphere kept swirling.

Knives maintained a steady beat on wooden chopping boards.

The tiny pieces kept vaporising into steam.

The animals were piece by piece vanishing.

I looked at the flesh being clinically sliced, and the blood, some of it still dribbling down the chopping board sides.

Other people in the kitchen, well, they just didn't see. They only noticed 'meat' and our meal coming together.

To them it was all just 'food'—mushrooms, capsicum, beef, ham, cheese … .

No difference.

No cattle, no pigs, no dairy cows.

Just food.

All just food.

A shudder ran though me and hairs on the back of my neck stood up.

It brought me round.

The instant was over.

No-one noticed a thing.

No-one saw the cows and pigs.

How could they?

It was all an imaginary moment thawed before my eyes, not a logical progression of publicly available thought projected over an extended time span.

Although that's how it felt.

As I re-entered reality I was again primed to spruik the virtues of being vegan and attack the inhumanity and ecological degradation associated with animal slaughter.

But before I could mount a soapbox, the carnage of all those butchered, overlooked 'meat' animals hit me.

Was I actually the only one aware of them, aware of the slaughter?

Surely not.

Life can be a foggy fantasy, I thought, but we each have our particular awareness.

Can the truth be just sliced up? I wondered.

和

Momentarily yes, and before some eyes permanently, but never forever for everyone, I felt.

Whether fleetingly vague or charmingly orchestrated, awareness is far from black and white.

There are degrees of everything, even murder.

It struck me to listen, not speak.

This is family I am again about to harangue, I said to myself.

I am helping prepare vegetables that will go on their meat pizzas as well as my holier-than-thou vegan ones.

Life, and death for that matter, are complicated but words, no matter how harsh, won't save animals tonight.

We are about to share a meal, as we have done so many times before, and hopefully many times to come.

Listen.

Listen to what's going on, inside my head and outside.

~~

How hypocritical am I!

That was the next thought.

Try as I might, I cannot escape where I come from.

I was once a meat eater and still depend on those around me for love and understanding to live with my latter day vegan tendencies, I reluctantly knew.

I have not purged myself of every skerrick of contact with the less enlightened.

That's impossible.

In the past though, expressing my righteous view had too frequently spilled over from opinion to a discourse driven by well intentioned zeal.

Luckily, at this moment my mouth did not open.

I remained cocooned in silence.

Stillness won the tug-a-war with my vocal cords.

What right had I to tell anyone what they should and should not eat or how to live their lives, I thought.

There must be a better way.

I sat quietly during that evening meal.

I heard a lot and let the conversation pitch and heave at will.

And a few things became clearer.

Life is layered. There is no one truth nor no one truth holder.

As long as we cooperated, vegan and meat eaters could more than coexist, we could gradually create a better world together, I thought.

Supper, in all its guises, would taste sweeter without some form of obligatory sermon.

I saw that life was a continuum of change through which we all moved at different rates.

And probably the most important thought—I understood that the occasion had finally arrived for me to weigh personal respect more heavily against confrontation.

I should look at what binds, rather than what blinds us.

和

Well, I should look at what blinds me anyway.

On this occasion I knew I didn't have to clobber anyone with my opinions on meat or anything for that matter.

Example could say more than words.

I must do more within me and criticise less, I thought.

I realised that the need for diversity in life was not actually an abstract concept to be applied to other people or objects.

It was not some patch of Amazon jungle, it was an inescapable and fundamental concept that applied to my most commonplace here and now.

Diversity, although painful at times, is essential.

Our strength actually lies in cooperation between people of vastly different persuasions.

These thoughts trickled through me like relief.

Then, later as we washed up, doubt also crept into the room.

Beside this feeling of ease I was left with two questions that seemed to contradict a cooperative approach.

'Why couldn't the world's decision-makers see the obvious connection between the personal health of mankind, reduced poverty, humane treatment of animals, international water security and other environmental benefits of being vegan?'

And secondly: 'Why couldn't I even convince my own family to see the animals they're eating, step past an academic understanding and actually be vegans day in, day out?'

I'd like to reach for a couple of quick and worry-free answers, but that would be blithely leaning towards a flat earth type of thinking.

I know no 'one size fits all' solution resolves anything of substance.

And I don't have all the answers I'd like, though that certainly would be nice.

While a more considered approach to these and associated questions may eventually include simple actions, most people need to get a better handle on what we are facing individually and globally before we could collectively turn on really effective action.

Effective action, that sounds like a packet of crusty crusader's weathered, dry biscuits.

Hopefully it doesn't have to be, I thought.

As the evening passed, my mind repeatedly returned to the importance of our kitchen.

It's our gathering space, overall a place of warmth and love.

Fairly regularly too it's also a place where conflict is aired as we confront or tiptoe round the clumsiness of human contact.

Kitchens are these type of communal gathering places everywhere.

和

Regardless of our ethnic groupings, they are places
where thought, word and deed can become one
with our most basic requirement for nourishment
on several levels.

And shared meals create a sacred space as they
ground us and help us cope with our own realities.

How could that goodwill be harnessed, I wondered?

So, in an attempt to unravel this conundrum, I'll draw
a backdrop sketch of where vegans come from.

Well, on second thought, that should come straight
after a glimpse at ninja, for there is a little of that
ilk in us all.

和

hidden menace
(forces from earth, fire, water and wind)

A dark figure creeps over rooftops, shadows a courtyard and slips into a building, undetected, as if straight through a wall. Too late, the faintest glint of steel is fingered by moonlight, and a person at its mercy in bed will not rise with the sun.

The weapon is sheathed and inconspicuous steps retraced.

This is a ninja in action.

He comes from Japan's feudal past.

He comes, some say, from clans that wreaked matchless terror.

Some say they are no more.

Ninja were medieval mercenaries of espionage, sabotage, arson and assassination, clad from head to toe in black when necessary to conceal a small arsenal of weapons, their martial arts prowess and intent.

They are cloaked now in mysticism and attributed with supernatural feats such as invisibility, flying, walking on water and being able to transform into animals.

Their origins and activities are obscured by time and folklore.

Some say their roots reach back more than 2000 years.

Parts of their story though have seeped through to the present, and these include aspects from which we may learn and continue to confidently adapt.

和

They were not merely heartless, indiscriminate murderers.

They were esoteric warriors, and remain so.

Names such as Tomo Sukesada, Fujibayashi Nagato, Mochizuki Chiyome, Ishikawa Goemon, Kato Danzo, Hattori Hanzo and their supposed exploits have, in some places, been enshrined.

Ninja flourished in a deadly age, rigorously trained under a code that tapped into natural law and developed purposeful physical, mental and spiritual strength.

In Japanese calligraphy, known as *kanji*, the written expression of ninja has two elements, *nin,* which means to hide and *ja,* which stands for person.

The most significant character is nin and while its original Chinese meaning was patience and endurance, in Japan it evolved into shinobi, to hide.

An oriental understanding of patience is a blade against our heart.

Nin has two parts, the upper is a blade with a long dot, as if it were a drop of blood falling from a sword, and the lower part is a heart.

The *ja* character is understood to be representative of an aged, wise and respected person.

Combination of the ninja characters aims to capture the balance between rest and motion, the secret of a silent and ethereal way.

As you can't knock on a ninja's front door today and ask—'Where did you come from, what exactly did you get up to, and why?'—it's impossible for all the facts of their activities to be laid bear before us.

It's just as impossible to unearth the first ninja's emergence.

Spies the world over have been around forever and although some ninja clans can formally trace their lineage back at least 500 years, much of what has been handed on from masters has been word of mouth.

Japanese legend has it that ninja descended from a demon that was half man and half crow.

More likely, they emerged as an opposing force to their upper-class contemporaries, the samurai.

China's Tang Dynasty was in decline during the late 800s, falling in the year 907 and igniting 50 years of chaos that caused some generals to flee across the sea to Japan.

They brought different military tactics and principles with them.

After 1020, Chinese monks also began escaping to Japan, bringing with them new medicines and fighting philosophies, many of which are understood to have originated in India and filtered through Tibet and China.

These monks taught Japan's warrior monks, the Yamabushi, and some commoners.

和

For more than a century, Chinese and native Japanese fighting tactics are understood to have blended into a sort of counter culture with few universal rules.

Around 1162 a samurai named Daisuke Togakure, who lost virtually everything and was disgraced when defeated in battle, was said to have been wandering the mountains near Honshu.

He met a Chinese warrior monk named Kain Doshi who had renounced his Bushido code. Doshi helped show Togakure a new way of viewing life and thus a means to move on.

The pair are said to have developed a type of guerilla warfare, that ultimately became known as ninjitsu.

Although the authenticity of various teachings remains in dispute, Togakure descendants are credited in some accounts as establishing the first formal ninja school.

~~

Ninja were street smart.

They used covert fighting methods while samurai openly had rules of combat honour, following the Bushido way.

In battle, a samurai would select a single opponent, announce a challenge, list their pedigree and attack.

But they could not always win.

So this is where ninja came in.

Samurai often hired them to do their dirty work—spying, conducting sneak attacks and even assassinations.

Samurai enemies also hired them, so ninja became a class both needed and feared.

While some ninja leaders were former samurai the vast majority of ordinary ninja were farmers and villagers who initially learned to fight for self-preservation.

Fundamentally, they developed techniques to survive a violent time of political and social turmoil.

Being drawn from the lower classes, literary interest in them was scarce during their peak years, and they were trained to be anonymous about their existence and actions.

They were taught forms of martial arts, staff and spear fighting, blade throwing, warring strategies and concealment.

Ninjitsu tactics were practical and many ninja weapons were modified farm implements, sickles, wood-cutting saws and pruning shears that, in themselves, would not give away their owner's identity.

They concocted poisons that were added to enemy food or administered by dart or blade.

Some ninja disguised themselves as flute playing mystics and used flutes as blow dart tubes or clubs.

和

As any espionage agent would confirm, ninja were not clothed in their sneaky dark costumes all the time, they usually dressed to blend with society and the ordinary lives they publicly portrayed.

And their hire fees helped transfer wealth to lower classes.

Ninja clans rose to major prominence between 1336 and 1600 when Japan was almost constantly at war with itself.

For more than 50 years from 1336 Japan had two separate imperial courts fighting to control the country and ninja worked for both sides, spying, infiltrating castles, burning down fortresses and such.

Then the Onin War broke out in 1467 and although it only lasted a decade, it ushered in a century of unrest, known as the Sengoku, or warring states period, that ran until 1568.

Ninja continued to be heavily involved in spying, agitating and destabilising in numerous ways, instigating surprise attacks and infiltrating enemy lines during sieges.

From the Sengoku period arose villages in Japan's Iga and Koga provinces devoted to ninja development.

These cradles of ninjitsu were remote, surrounded by mountains and their training schools produced professional ninja hired mostly by opposing Japanese nobility in their power struggles.

In addition to their shady espionage activities, there are accounts of Iga and Koga ninja through the years acting as bodyguards, gardeners, police, protectors of palace and inner castle compounds and even fighting alongside regular military troops.

Ninja were born into their profession.

They were coached from early childhood in traditions secretly passed within families.

As well as martial arts disciplines, youth studied survival and scouting techniques, poisons and explosives, long distance running, climbing, stealth methods of swimming and walking, teamwork, professions required for disguise and a degree of medicinal information.

Although years of rugged ninja training were Spartan, this did not extinguish initiative, in fact quick wits were nourished as they alone could keep them alive on some secret missions.

Rare documents indicate foretelling of the future and cosmology were used to instruct on ideal times for certain actions.

Ninja had charms and incantations associated with Buddhist gods, Taoist mythology and the Shinto religion and used unusual hand gestures in spiritual, healing and exorcism rituals and allegedly to transform themselves into other things and even cast spells to immobilise opponents.

和

As formal ninjitsu schools developed, disciplines said to be definitive of all ninjitsu schools came to be.

These included spiritual refinement, unarmed combat, sword, staff and spear techniques, meteorology, geography, disguise, concealment, escape and spying tactics.

Counter measures to thwart ninja also became common.

Precautions against assassinations included hiding weapons in toilets or under removable floorboards.

Buildings were constructed with traps and trip wires attached to alarm bells.

Japanese castles were designed to be difficult to navigate with winding routes leading to inner compounds. Holes in walls provided surveillance of their labyrinthine paths, floors resting on metal hinges were designed to squeak when walked over, grounds were gravel covered to warn of intruders and segregated buildings improved sabotage fire containment.

During the sixteenth century several war lords, rose who were relentless foes of Buddhism and Yamabushi monks, including Oda Nobunga.

After several ninja attempts on his life, in November 1581, Nobunaga invaded the Iga province with an army, said to be of about 46,000 men, and attacked a combined ninja force of fewer than 4000.

In less than a week, large numbers of ninja were slain and survivors scattered to other provinces throughout the country.

Some were later able to find political service but as the Edo period brought peace and stability to Japan from 1603 to 1868 they basically stepped into history.

What is believed to be a final record of ninja employed in open warfare occurred during the Shimabara Rebellion, in the two years from 1637, when they were recruited by a shogun (military dictator) to fight Christian rebels who made a stand in Hara Castle.

The fall of Hara Castle ended the rebellion, forced Christianity in Japan underground and provided the last written mention of ninja in war.

Early in the eighteenth century another shogun formed an intelligence agency that was involved in collecting information on nobles and government officials.

The secret nature of his 'oniwabanshu', or garden keepers, and earlier custom of using Iga and Koga clan members as palace groundsmen has led some people to define them as ninja even though there is said to be no written link with ninja, who were also known as shinobi.

So now, real ninja have faded into obscurity.

But what could they offer contemporary times?

和

A great deal, for instance, dedication to honing our physical, mental and spiritual wellbeing amid today's breathtaking distractions wouldn't go astray for most of us.

Much underlies the ninja legend but I feel the essence of ninja success appears to be in the art of surprise, catching people unaware rather than applying brute force.

They readied themselves then observed before exploiting the natural environment and often used simple tricks and people's weaknesses and inattention to outsmart bigger and more numerous opponents.

お庭番衆

oniwabanshu
(garden keeper)

Yes they could be violent, but feuding was the hallmark of feudal times, not an abnormal trait.

Unlike us, they did not evolve in a period of manicured McMansions, internet cafes, social welfare and superannuation.

In Japan's feudal era, peasants comprised about 80 percent of the population.

They lived in poverty, were tied to the land, restricted to growing rice and forced by lords using the specialised class of well equipped warriors, the samurai, to ensure payment of up to 50 percent of their harvests as land tax.

In addition, peasants faced numerous miscellaneous taxes such as charges on female children, the popular drink sake, beans, cloth and hemp and were also used as labour on roads, bridges and other public facilities such as horse stations on main roads.

Ninja became a force for the downtrodden.

While not advocating violence today, I believe there are ninja traits in everyone.

Who doesn't harbour anti-establishment sentiment at times, want to right a wrong or dream of winning some battle against insurmountable odds?

Who amongst us does not know anger?

It is with everyone on a small and large scale.

It is an undeniable part of human nature.

Our privilege of birth largely influences whether or not we face the gravest dangers and have to make a choice whether or not to fire a real shot in anger.

My father Frank, for instance, lived most of his 91 years last century and at one stage wound up as an Australian airman in World War II.

Late in the conflict, dad was a wireless operator/air gunner flying over Germany in a plane dropping aluminium strips to muddle the Luftwaffe radar, bombs to destroy military targets and running 'spoof' raids to divert enemy attention from other allied aircraft.

和

He was among the lucky 50 per cent of aircrew to walk away from those Halifaxes in the end.

While savouring the comradeship of his mates he was 'scared witless' peering through his little glass window on those night raids over Germany and viewed war as a waste of life and resources that did not necessarily resolve the problem at hand.

My dad did what he did because of what he believed the era demanded of him.

From an early age I told him I would never go to war.

I couldn't.

Of course I spoke then, as I do now, from a platform of prosperous peace in Australian history which has flowed from overcoming past upheavals.

I know war is ugly, and sometimes it's unavoidable, a necessary evil.

Is it ever worth it?

I'd like to say no, but the answer is not that black and white, I believe we (our species) have to do our utmost to find a way around it.

My perspective though is not universal.

Even so, surely it's a universal desire that all people, all sentient beings in fact, could live in prosperous peace.

I hope a similar driving desire burned within ninja as they did what they did in the belief of what their era demanded of them.

They had to apply themselves to a feudal reality.

Thankfully, that brutality is not in our faces today, but when we consider things such as the inequities between some peoples, and the way some of us abuse our good fortune, we have much room for improvement.

From a vegan perspective, for me, a ninja approach equates to taking a clever, tactical line through life rather than being a bull at a gate.

Paradoxically, there is freedom in discipline, if it's thoughtful.

Hardship has always been a regular component of life.

Learn from it.

We must seek our own practical truths in all aspects of endeavour and then hold strong to our convictions with an open mind that relies on intuition.

As we develop discipline we apply this learning, with empathy, to others and ourselves and should not think we have all the answers.

Ninja were guided in practical ways by the four elements—earth, fire, water and wind.

Learn from these elements what it means to be grounded in reality (earth), harness passion when confronted (fire), flow toward your goals (water) and change direction when circumstances dictate (wind).

和

Being ninja smart is not about scoring high on an intelligence quota chart.

Ninja integrated mind and body awareness, sharpened natural instincts and acted unconventionally to accomplish the seemingly impossible.

My enabling ninja move is in embracing my imperfect human attachment to all that's around me as I ruthlessly attempt to tread a compassionate way.

Is that contradictory?

No, it's a determined course guided by continuing correction from what feels right.

To live intently, lean towards simplicity and perceptively take a lifelong path of self-mastery while being as connected as possible to each pebble on the journey, each living thing along the way—that's my hope.

You see, not only vices are contagious, nor all that is contagious a vice.

As the Oriental saying goes, we must learn to feed the right tiger.

The vegan tiger, I say.

和

1924
(donald's realisation)

In 1924 a sensitive 14-year-old English boy walked up to his mum and dad and announced his New Year's resolution—he would no longer be eating meat.

It was a stunning statement by young Donald Watson, but one he had to make.

There was no alternative.

Donald felt he must respond to an inner conviction even though no-one he knew followed vegetarian precepts.

Donald realised that the meat in his meals was actually the farmyard animals he had come to love.

He could not eat his friends.

That's what it came down to.

His parents did not understand.

Yorkshire was a coalmining community and people here did not get by on a vegetable diet.

Donald explained his position again.

His parents eventually accepted it and said they would support his decision.

Years later Donald publicly spoke of that time.

As a child he used to visit his Uncle George's farm where he was surrounded by interesting animals.

'They all gave something,' said Donald.

和

'The farm horse pulled the plough, the lighter horse pulled the trap, the cows gave milk, the hens gave eggs and the cockerel was a useful alarm clock. I didn't realise at the time he had another function too.

'The sheep gave wool. I could never understand what the pigs gave, but they seemed such friendly creatures, always glad to see me,' Donald said.

Soon though he lay hold of Uncle George's purpose for pigs when he saw one slaughtered.

By now, Donald had also seen animals being pushed through doors beside a local butcher's shop.

'I once saw a cow and calf enter together,' he said.

'I wondered later which one the butcher killed first.

'On one occasion I actually watched a cow being killed at an abattoir in a field where local children were free to watch and where they hoped to be given a bladder to use as a football,' he said.

Donald's parents encouraged their three children to set their own paths and Donald reacted to the surrounding industrial and farming landscape by developing a reverence for the countryside.

He observed nature and his view of this balanced order and its universal life force provided a platform on which to continually examine mankind's relationship with all flora and fauna.

At 15 he left school to become an apprentice joiner.

By 20 he had gained a skilful passion for woodwork and so began teaching the subject.

Then, meeting like-minded folk in the Leicester Vegetarian Society, Donald expanded his interest in education, organic gardening and hiking on the moors.

Giving up the use of all animal products was a reasoned extension of his thinking.

Now he was 32.

Being a pacifist, he registered as a conscientious objector to World War II and faced the toughest questioning, by others, of his ethical position.

To kill his fellow man was unthinkable, despite international hostilities and people all over the world not having similar clarity.

He was buoyed, however, by his older brother and younger sister becoming vegetarian, non-smokers, teetotallers and conscientious objectors.

In 1944 Donald gathered together some friends with pure vegetarian intentions, formed a society and set about finding a word to describe their way of life.

That year, he and wife, Dorothy, eventually settled on 'vegan'.

It came from the first three letters, and last two, of the word vegetarian.

As Donald explained in a media interview later in life: 'Because veganism starts with vegetarianism and carries it through to its logical conclusion.'

和

By departing from society's conforming standards, and mainstream medical advice, he felt a general level of disapproval was ever present.

Donald said: 'The kindest criticism we received was that we meant well, or that the sheer problems arising from choosing to live in a world catering mainly for other people would get us down in the end.

'Other critics said, "it seems to suit you" without realising that it might suit them too if only they would try it'.

Donald admitted that the vegan society was like most other groups.

'Of course, we did not always agree on everything. We argued for a long time about whether members should sign a pledge, before deciding against it,' Donald said.

Debate on whether to eat honey was also protracted and ended with a decision not to.

'The society soon widened its aims to include all animal exploitation, in brief, to work for a new relationship with the rest of sentient creation in a symbiotic relationship, if possible to live and help live rather than just live and let live,' he said.

As the vegan movement crept around the world Donald didn't seek recognition for the pivotal part he played in its grounding.

He largely sidestepped public attention, simply being pleased to see the vision for a more compassionate way of life in harmony with nature become reality for so many.

While considering himself 'a practical man with both feet firmly on the ground' Donald was pleased to confound critics who thought his diet would ruin his health.

Donald died peacefully at home in Keswick, England, in November 2005, two weeks after his 95th birthday.

He was a gentleman in the true sense of the word. Strong-willed and persistent, yes, and his thoughtful approach to life helped establish the modern vegan concept and set a tone for its wider acceptance.

I'm not saying Donald was the first vegan.

He was among the first to be called vegan and his life and writings helped introduce the concept to a broad cross-section of society.

Many earlier people have lived under similar regimes, I'm sure.

History records vegetarian diets of several types, in various parts of the world, throughout all ages.

Can anyone recall a bloke from ancient history named Plato for instance?

This Greek philosopher, who kicked about 400 years before Jesus Christ wore sandals, lived a no-meat lifestyle.

和

To what extent, no-one knows with utter certainty, but some of his words on such a lifestyle have come through to today along with many of his other influential thoughts.

Plato was a student of the renowned Socrates, and Plato went on to teach the also renowned thinker Aristotle.

This trio laid the foundation for philosophy in today's western society.

I wouldn't put Donald Watson quite in the same boat as these three wise men, but in his own modest way Donald did further the efforts of those who came before him.

He lived his convictions and made a difference.

On second thoughts, perhaps Donald should be named in such company as he rose above his station and contributed meaningfully to life in an enduring and potentially earth-saving way.

In an interview two years before he died, Donald said he had never used medicines 'orthodox or fringe'.

He also dismissed genetic inheritance as the reason for his longevity.

'My father died of a coronary at 63. Neither his father nor grandfather reached 70 despite the fact that as farmers they had plenty of fresh air, exercise and organic foods. On my mother's side, all died around the age of 70,' he said.

When asked for advice he would give anyone considering the transition to being vegetarian and then vegan he said: 'Don't leave it too long.'

Donald Watson appears to have recognised early that a life of compassion was also one of compromise.

This is not a bad thing.

It's practical.

Donald did not yield on his personal lifestyle stance, he just had to accept that widespread inhumane treatment of animals and degradation of the environment would continue.

He chose to reduce his angst and work to convert others to his ways by explaining what he was on about and showing them through his actions.

That peaceful determination would be handy.

Sometimes it's easier to get cranky.

Too often in the past I have been niggled by what has happened around me, at close quarters and most distant.

I try to be mindful that the adjustment of conflicting views takes time and the settlement of differences is best achieved through respect and mutual concession.

But I have found it hard.

It can be tough to alter our own habits, customs and beliefs, harder still to change the world's, and impossible to do it by yourself.

和

While it is correct, that we can't save the world single handedly, many of us are overwhelmed by that thought.

It is familiar for all of us to feel infinitesimally small when confronted by serious social issues.

We're convinced how little one ordinary person could do.

The fact that certain things are inevitable, outside our abilities or controlled by greater forces seems to have been drummed into us from a very early age.

So how often do we back off some matters of importance before striking a genuine blow?

It's easier not to see what's staring us in the face, to fail through avoidance as it were, than succeed.

There's less risk, less effort, the outcome is predictable and excuses aren't hard to find.

Perseverance is worth it, although ultimate success can be difficult.

It's oft measured by others differently to us, and we usually don't meet all necessary criteria.

I'd say having a go at something difficult is actually success because it overcomes anxiety of the unknown, the fear of failure that too often underpins our inertia.

~~

Focus on what we can do rather than what we can't, let alone whether or not any results may win a Pulitzer Prize.

Through the years it has become evident to me when faced by a stumbling block that the only way to deal with it was to work out a way to dismantle it into pieces.

Break it down into manageable bits.

When questions are too hard to answer, it's often the case that we're asking the wrong question or thinking about our conclusion the wrong way.

Take a breath and try looking from a different angle.

I accept we all have limitations, but it's also a fact that most problems can be brought down to a size which anyone can eyeball.

This approach may not enable an entire issue to be licked, but even the thought of one forward step can help lift a person's feet for real movement.

By breaking things down, we are all able to do a lot more than most of us initially consider possible.

Ingrained food choices, for instance, have not been permanently set in stone by the dictates of conventional wisdom.

They can be confronted and altered to become a solid plank in a raft of actions with wide-ranging and ongoing positive personal and environmental outcomes.

Predictably, by that I mean vegan alternatives.

There are three prime underlying reasons why people take up a vegan lifestyle.

Well, I don't see it as a 'lifestyle' as such, I believe it's more a complete way of living.

和

It's a thoughtful and changing process rather than a shallow activity attached to popular trends, particular foods or fleeting displays to create an impression.

The three reasons are that it includes a healthy diet, it is based on humane ethics and it reduces environmental degradation.

It's amazing to realise what is good for an individual is also great for our planet, and all its coinheritors.

For me, veganism is the merging of practicality, spirituality, philosophy and faith.

It took me many years to arrive here.

It is a great deal more than not eating animals, saying 'no' to dairy products, eggs and honey, refusing to stomp on pesky snails in our vegetable garden or giving old leather shoes to a charity.

It's about our whole being, as mortal and impaired as it is.

And it feels so assuring.

The vegan concept fosters deliberate action through a deep and enduring conscience.

It is about life's journey, social justice, meaningful interaction and facing our own perpetual adjustments by trying to balance idealism and realism.

Agile thought comes from attention to detail, without being trapped in it.

Motivation, based on natural instincts, becomes increasingly self-driven, even if it's not in line with what other people 'know' to be right.

And while all that resonates confidence, it's hardly a set and forget matter.

I think I'll always understand a wander on shaky ground.

Confronting my own failings remains a fairly firm obstacle.

And I don't think I'm Robinson Crusoe on this point.

Righteousness I find hard to shake.

Killing and eating animals is wrong.

No two ways about it.

I'm right with that.

It's not complex.

But I also see that such indignation directed at others is a blunt implement that causes more harm than good.

I need to keep working on it.

To temper the steel.

As strange as it seems, strength can be found in vulnerability, acknowledging our limitations tends to quench our arrogance.

Again, I'd like to break things down to manageable bits.

So to scratch at the root of a meat-based diet, and the intricacies of its impacts, light needs to be cast on the carcasses buried at humanity's feet.

Let's look at why people eat the animals with whom we share our land and waterways.

和

taking stock
(why humans eat animals)

It seems to me that meat eating comes down to one base thing—habit.

Plain and simple.

Convenient consumption has been passed from one generation to the next, largely defying any penetrating questions amid our affluent and often cluttered lives.

It's what wealthy humans do.

It's habit borne of our bullyboy survival of the fittest origins.

Our industrialised society makes it so easy.

And it's cheered on by marketing propaganda and price.

All morals are heavily influenced by image and our wallets.

People behind the meat trade have successfully worked on human habit to expand it into a growing addiction for society.

Meat eating has become a thoughtless process, an ingrained dietary default for those who see themselves as sophisticated, successful and aspiring.

Truthfully though, killing animals for our eating pleasure, is not a human survival necessity.

People who accept it's a nutritional necessity are romanticising themselves. And that's putting it mildly.

Yes, meat can satisfy a physical hunger, although these days clever promotion largely helps meat eaters fulfil an egotistical status hunger.

And the consequences?

How many people simply don't see the consequences?

和

Most of us.

Meat eating is unceasingly reinforced by media advertising which has bestowed it with a nutritional and social prosperity well beyond its actual worth.

It has long been commercially pushed as an essential protein food and an integral part of a vibrant, modern life.

By endowing it with such rank the general community has been led to believe that meat eating is part of expressing who we are, or more precisely, who we really would like to be.

It confirms the human position, on top of the food chain.

And convenience is the hook that carcasses hang on.

Meat is just so hassle-free to get hold of and for most 'civilised' people it's relatively financially cheap.

But ultimately, for most people, a crucial connection has been severed.

How many meat eaters consider the animals they munch on having recently been living sentient beings?

Very few, if any, I'd say.

Who cares?

Everyone's flat out, usually attempting to squash too many things into their daily domestic, social and work requirements.

Sadly, a limited number of people have time to regard meat for what it actually is—the flesh and other vital parts of dead animals that do not deserve to be specifically bred, confined and killed for our short-sighted culinary desires.

Numerous factors prop up the meat eating habit.

Traditional religion has even contributed to eroding our sensitivities to the industry's death and destruction.

My mother Mary, for instance, saw meat as an indispensible dietary requirement rather than exploitation of another species.

And she didn't see fish as animals at all.

'Even though they live, breathe and swim in water before they get onto your plate?' I asked her.

'That's right, they're fish,' she said.

'But they have a mum and dad, like me, and all other animals from koalas to beef cows.'

'Fish are fish, not beef cows.'

'So they're not meat—just like carrots, potatoes and strawberries, I suppose?'

'They're not meat, like cows.'

'They're just seafood, with the emphasis on food?'

'They're not meat, they're fish Paul!'

'Mum?'

'Paul!'

That's how our last conversation on the subject ended ages ago.

和

It was in the year 2000 in fact.

While it made as little sense then as it does now we could both see the futility of pursuing the discussion further, although later that day mum said that even if people considered fish to be meat, it was 'different' to other meat.

It was acceptable to eat all sorts of meat, in fact, we needed it to stay healthy, she claimed.

Now I'm not going to psychoanalyse my mum here.

In her defence though I will say she lived a full life as a normal intelligent and healthy person, being a primary school teacher, hard-working wife and mother of eight children.

Despite some common human imperfections, and her memory being devoured by dementia in the end, she was always a person of unconditional love.

She helped me understand that the universe has a range of definite powers and subtle nuances beyond my comprehension.

Not that we were in agreement, mind you, on exactly what they all were.

And she always held a faith backed by unshakable beliefs.

Mum was raised under Catholic tenets that included the doctrine that you didn't eat meat on Fridays.

You ate fish.

Right or wrong, we all know many people with similar settled views on one thing or another.

They respect certain conventions, have no regular need to question them and certainly don't want the likes of me poking my nose into their business.

Which leads me to chooks (chicken or poultry as the politically correct call them).

Chooks are a lot like fish in the popular mindset.

Usually it's not until people are asked about eating chicken flesh do they regard chooks as ever being living, breathing animals.

And even then this 'white' meat is somehow (as my mum would say) 'different' from 'red' meat.

As if it's not really dead animal pieces on their plates.

On a day to day basis these people just have no reason to consider that they're devouring anything they shouldn't.

People don't see millions of hapless chooks crammed by the tens of thousands into huge tin sheds, let alone the climate changing gases from copious amounts of manure and waste the poultry industry generates, or the water, electricity and transport fossil fuel it consumes.

Our community has been conditioned to block out thoughts of animals being killed to eat so most of us recognise meat only for what is right before us at dinner.

It's just food.

和

Meat's 'benefits' have been so repeated that most people unconsciously believe industry claptrap that it's a nutritional prerequisite for their existence.

Where it comes from is not of mainstream interest.

Whether it's chicken, fish, beef or whatever, for the majority, meat is nothing more than a product that comes from refrigerated supermarket cabinets.

Right.

These people have been caged by an insidious ignorance.

And the link between animals and other consumer products such as milk, cheese, butter, eggs, honey, leather shoes, belts, handbags and lounge chairs in the family home has become even more tenuous.

Really, how strange is it that dairy products, for instance, have become a substantial ingredient in human health?

Again, we can thank successful propaganda for the prejudice.

Cow's milk is secreted through the mammary glands of cows and is naturally intended for the weight gain of baby cows.

Yet here we are, a different species of animal, lapping it up as if it were vital for our wellbeing.

Advertising marketeers, with cartoon rural settings painted on the side of their trucks, have created a blissful unquestioning disposition amongst us.

Pervasive widespread conventional 'thinking' is now straight forward.

Meat and other consumer products from animals are a 'normal' part of our 'normal' world—undeniably necessary.

The pace of our lives also supports this ignorant, selfish mentality.

During my generation, food of all kinds has been virtually inexhaustible in Australia, in fact pretty much throughout western society.

It presents no reason for the populace to wonder how it continually stocks those supermarket shelves.

Commercial propagandists relentlessly extend and entrench the view that meat is an elemental human requirement.

The subversive ninja in society, anyone in fact who questions the norm, would have to be deluded in some way, and clearly an enemy of a stable economy.

They're radicals.

This basic argument has struck a common cord.

We all understand it can be easier to settle in and go with the flow.

Don't rock the boat, or be a wowser.

Don't be an extremist.

If you want to fit in, don't remind anyone of the slaughter, the pollution or the human health implications.

和

Perhaps though, some settled views would loosen up if people took the time to consider what lay beneath so much of our daily expanding consumerism.

But why would they?

Firstly, where would they find the time?

Time is short for us all, and who doesn't function best in their own comfort zone routines?

Granted, I have to concede that I'm settled in many of my views these days.

Astonishingly so on occasions.

And meat eating is a prime example.

I'm comfortably, without question, opposed to it.

It is an exceedingly destructive and violent practice in so many ways and completely superfluous for a healthy human diet, regardless of how anyone garnishes a pro-meat argument.

I also feel ashamed when I pause and think about what we humans do to other animals.

Absolute shame.

Categorise me as an abolitionist if you want.

A ban on meat eating is certainly a policy I now easily apply to myself and would love to see applied generally.

But, as I noted earlier, life is a continuum.

While most people attempt to be morally consistent, our morality is part of a progression.

I remember as a young teenager being disgusted by having to eat meat with great big blood vessels running through it.

Yuck!

But there was no option.

From the earliest of days my parents expected me to eat everything on my plate.

There was limited debate.

None really.

I complied.

Despite the edict though, the sight, taste and thought of those bloody vessels began long ago to sour my estimation of meat eating.

Looking back I see that having to eat against my will played a role in my rebellion of authority and the gradual dawning that I really was responsible for the way I conducted my life.

That included what I ate and how I felt about the production of meat.

I will step back from a blow by blow description of the way animals end up as neatly wrapped little packets of chilled cuisine or what they endure to become other consumer products.

Suffice to say, it is a tad indelicate as table talk.

Please consider the enormity of the situation though.

Our global human population is expanding so fast we're expected to exceed nine billion by 2050.

That's about two billion more than today.

And so few years off.

和

Our worldwide livestock industry already kills millions upon millions of animals every day.

Statistics can be rubbery, so while the following figures are as accurate as I could find they should be treated as approximations because killing counts vary and so do data collection methods.

In North America alone 500,000 animals are killed every hour.

The United Kingdom's slaughterhouses account for more than 600 million a year.

Based on our human population, a comparable number of animals are killed in Australia.

In the state of New South Wales alone more than 12million cattle, calves, pigs, sheep, lambs, goats and deer, plus about 150 million chooks, are slaughtered for human consumption each year.

Despite a widespread perception that the dairy industry is outside this brutality, the Australian dairy industry alone sentences more than 700,000 young male 'bobby' calves to death for meat each year as they are 'useless' for milk production.

A spokeswoman for Australia's first meat free week in March 2013, Melissa Dixon, said that with an average of 120 kilograms of meat consumed by every man, woman and child in the nation every year, Australians were the second biggest meat eaters in the world, after Americans.

Such consumption was not possible without factory farming which caused suffering to more than 500 million animals in Australia each year, she said.

Factory farming is the number one cause of animal cruelty today, with two thirds of the world's meat coming from large scale industrial operations were animals were treated like production line commodities with their pain and distress being disregarded in the pursuit of profit, Ms Dixon said.

A prime example of such cruelty was revealed by a 2013 Australian federal court case involving three major chicken and egg producing companies and a marketing claim that chooks were 'free to roam'.

The case judge visited their sheds and found that with an average of 30,000 to 40,000 chooks per shed this amounted to about 20 birds to every square metre.

So for much of their 42-day lifespan the chooks lived in an area roughly the size of an A4 sheet of paper and were constantly pressed upon by other chooks.

Yes, you read correctly, the entire life of all these chooks has been cut down to 42 days to satisfy mankind's meat eating madness.

Also, the world's commercial fisheries are collapsing as there is not enough aquatic life in the seas to meet human's ravenous expectations, according to Captain Paul Watson, the controversial founder

和

of the marine protection group Sea Shepherd and co-founder of the peak environmental body Greenpeace.

In 2001, humans ate about 230 million tonnes of animal carcasses, and at the current appetite growth rate that consumption will double, to 465 million tonnes by 2050.

This expanding demand is a major factor causing global deforestation, increasing biodiversity threats, massive water use and pollution, overgrazing, land compaction and erosion problems.

The livestock sector is responsible for 18 per cent of the world's greenhouse gas pollution, less than the power industry, but worse than all the world's cars, planes and other forms of transport added together, according to The United Nations Food and Agriculture Organisation's 2006 report *Livestock's Long Shadow*.

Other sources have accused the meat and dairy industries of producing nearly 51 per cent of the world's greenhouse gases.

Captain Watson said that half the ocean plunder was ground up as fish meal and fed to cows, pigs, sheep, chickens and other animals destined to become meat meals for humans.

'We have turned the domestic cow into the largest marine predator on the planet. House cats consume more fish, especially tuna, than all the world's seals,' he said.

Microbiologist author Richard Lacey is also concerned about mankind's practice of recycling the remains of 'unwanted' animals, birds, and even some domestic pets, into stock feed.

In his book *Hard to swallow*, Professor Lacey describes it as 'effectively cannibalism'.

Land clearing for animal pasture is the biggest contributing factor to Australia's natural habitat destruction. Australia is wiping out animal species at a higher rate than every other country in the world, except for the United States of America—the land of plenty.

And some statistics even show Australia tops America in the species extinction stakes.

There are more than 1200 plant species and almost 350 animal species, including mammals, birds, reptiles, fish, frogs and insects on Australia's endangered lists.

Up to 50,000 litres of water are used to produce one kilogram of beef.

Rice, by comparison, uses 2500 litres for each kilogram.

Based on an average Australian diet, 90 per cent of household water use is 'indirect consumption', that means it is used producing all sorts of food, rather than flushing it down the toilet, having showers, watering the lawn or washing the duco of our lovely cars.

和

So, those of us inhabiting the earth's driest continent could save more of this precious life-giving liquid by going vegan than plugging up all the taps in our homes.

Reducing meat eating could also deal a blow against international poverty and malnutrition.

While enough grain is grown to feed every person on earth, most of it is used to feed animals for meat, dairy and egg production.

Of all the meat animals, cattle alone consume enough food to feed the entire human population.

This demand has helped push the price of grain out of reach for many poor people seeking the smallest amount of food to survive.

Australians, and others living in wealthy developed countries, have an obesity epidemic because of overeating, particularly processed foods laced with sugar, salt and fat, while people in developing, or 'third world', countries often can't get enough sustenance.

Of about 800 million people worldwide believed to be undernourished, more than 25,000 children younger than five starve or die in poverty every single day.

Every single day.

That's 25,000 children.

Okay, it might be simplistic to imply that you would save the life of any particular animal or even a particular fellow human by not eating meat for tea tonight.

That may be so, but it would certainly be moving in the right direction.

Reduced meat eating, even by just one person, must save life at some stage.

And that means particular human individuals, even if you or I do not know them personally or have been within cooee of their so called 'third world' countries.

Waste is another major impact.

The United Nations Food and Agriculture Organisation director Jose Graziano da Silva said in January 2013 that about 300 million tonnes of food in industrialised nations was wasted each year.

This was enough to feed the estimated 830 million people worldwide who went hungry.

The waste was more than all the food produced in sub-Saharan Africa and was estimated to be worth more than $955 billion dollars, each year, Mr Graziano da Silva said.

While much waste results from harvesting and distribution problems, such as storing food in difficult climatic conditions and unreliable harvests, retailers and consumers also shared the blame, he said.

But who really is to blame when the enormity of the situation is laid out?

和

We all are.

Although the use of the word blame allows us to shift responsibility, away from us as individuals, into an undefined social, governmental and corporate arena where someone else will deal with it.

That is delusion—an excuse for inaction.

I am dead sure that if substantial global change to reduce waste or move from meat-based to a vegan style of living was to succeed, it would come from what happens around kitchen tables.

Tables like yours, mine and our nextdoor neighbours.

Real change is a grassroots matter, whether it's sparked in our kitchens or not.

It has to intimately touch us all.

Eventually, it reaches past individuals to push every aspect of social, civic and economic interaction.

Strong leadership in politics, business, you name it, it's all driven by an underlying structure—the mundane daily actions of ordinary people.

That's why having us all consider the benefits of mankind eating less meat is an important starting point.

Even if I cannot nail down precisely what every single benefit may be, the statistics I've just rattled off highlight a few.

In my part of the world, when someone's close attention is drawn to the question of meat in their diet it is usually because of an increased awareness of health, or sickness concerns in their immediate family.

Our risk of obesity, heart disease, blood pressure, numerous cancers and many other medical issues generally goes hand on fork with eating meat and animal products, plus sitting on our butts too much.

和

what exactly is meat?
(more than offal)

Meat is much more than the flesh of animals used as food.

Any part of an animal carcass except a foetus, the unborn young from a mother's womb, can be eaten as meat in Australia.

That is law.

It means that virtually all the non-bony bits of dead cattle, sheep, pigs, poultry, goats, rabbits, camels and buffalo can legally be our mealtime fare.

While the Australian Federal Government's primary definition does not cover beasts slaughtered in the wild, the nation's individual state and territory regulations skip round this by allowing any animal to be eaten.

Fish and eggs come under separate national food categories.

All cold-blooded aquatic species, with and without a spinal column, including shellfish, can be eaten.

Under national rules frogs and other amphibians, plus lizards and other reptiles are excluded, but again the policy of state and territory decision-makers allow all species to be eaten.

Eggs, all the reproductive body from the shells of any bird, can be eaten as food.

Eggs comprise albumen jelly, membranes, the embryo sac and reproductive cells capable of being developed into new individuals.

(And while we're on chook eggs, their yolk is one of the heaviest concentrations of animal fat on earth.)

和

The national food standard describes meat flesh as the skeletal muscle of a slaughtered animal along with any attached fat, nerve, connective tissue, blood, blood vessel and rind.

That covers things such as ears, snouts, tongues and all the other flabby bits and appendages you can think of.

The internal organs of animals can also be included in meat and meat products.

Meat industry representatives lump this stuff under the cute title of 'offal'.

Offal includes brain, heart, blood, kidney, pancreas, liver, spleen, tongue, stomach and thymus.

A thymus is a glandular body or ductless gland of uncertain function found near the base of the neck in vertebrate species, including humans.

The meat industry's description for a thymus is 'sweetbread'.

More cute wordsmithing, eh.

Bone, bone marrow and meat flesh are not considered offal.

The law allows all types of offal to be eaten if it is noted on a food label, either as offal or its specific type, such as a pig's tongue for instance.

No prize for guessing the description commonly used.

Offal is okay in food not requiring a label in Australia as long as the seller somehow tells the buyer.

So, if you see or hear of food containing sweetbread, for instance, you now know it is not really bread and while I may never have tasted the stuff, I venture to say it's probably not very sweet either.

It's offal.

Some processed meat products need only contain 30 per cent meat.

And the stuff inside a meat pie needs only include 25 per cent meat to pass food standards.

Pies are interesting little things, don't you think?

They are known to have been eaten in Sydney since the mid 1800s, then hawked from the back of horse-drawn carts and sold over hotel counters.

They have been mass produced since the early 1900s.

Meat pies have risen from a takeaway snack ranking to become an inseparable part of Australian cuisine and national icon dish in many households, mainly through their association with football.

Advertising and lobbying have helped maintain the pie's resilience to bad press.

For example, in 2002 New South Wales premier Bob Carr, when launching a childhood obesity conference, said feeding youngsters a diet of meat pies, sausage rolls and chiko rolls (processed savoury meat snacks) was akin to child cruelty.

His remark attracted some heavy political fire from meat industry lobbyists.

和

Next year, when Mr Carr was no longer premier, he was reported by the media in a much more complimentary frame of mind.

He then viewed pies as a national Australian dish.

Also in 2002, the Australian Consumers Association studied 22 frozen meat pies available in supermarkets. (There's not much up to date public information available, that I could find, on what's in pies.)

Three brands, in 2002, did not have the minimum 25 per cent meat content, while their fat levels ranged from 15 grams to 35 grams in every pie.

Another study by the association four years later found five of 23 brands failed the minimum meat content test.

And in 2010 at least one of 20 brands still failed the 25 per cent test.

It made me wonder what the other 75 per cent of a 'meat' pie actually was.

But despite concerns in some quarters, Australians have generally stuck to meat pies like flies at a barbecue.

Now, the Australian population has grown to 22 million, and pie eating has increased to more than 500 million of the pastries every year.

Sausages are another of Australia's heavily consumed meaty products.

The national meat standard says sausages pass muster as food if half their filling is 'fat-free' meat flesh.

As much as 25 per cent of every sausage can be fat.

And although I'm no gambler, on this point I'd confidently punt a juicy green apple against the Sydney Harbour Bridge that the fat in sausages was likely to be crunched up pieces of animals.

Any artificial colouring agents can be applied to the surface of any meat or meat product without having to be declared on any label.

Additionally, Australian meat standards are only concerned about one disease fatal to humans— bovine spongiform encephalopathy, which we ordinary folk know as 'mad cow disease'.

But, I believe, the standard's mad cow filter is flimsy, to say the least.

It does not even apply to dairy products from bovines.

This means it does not apply to milk, butter, cheese and other products from cows, goats or similar animals.

The food standard's disease filter also does not apply to any meat or meat products containing gelatine from bovine skins or hides or collagen from bovine skins or hides.

This means sausage casings, for instance, don't even have to be mad cow disease checked.

和

The national standard's mad cow screen only applies to bovine fats and bovine tallow if they make up more than 30 per cent of a processed product.

Proteins in the brain tissue of animals with mad cow disease could cause the deadly Creutzfeldt Jakob Disease in humans who eat meat from these animals.

And a report in the *2009 Journal of Alzheimer's Disease* indicates that farmed fish may be increasing this risk as farmed fish are fed 'by-products' rendered from cows.

An article in the journal by Kentucky University neurologist Robert Friedland and his colleagues, titled *Bovine spongiform encephalopathy and aquaculture*, said fish consumption was widely recommended to humans as a source of omega-3 fatty acids which are said to reduce cardiovascular and Alzheimers diseases.

The article goes on to say: 'We are concerned that consumption of farmed fish may provide a means of transmission of infectious prions (particles) from cows with bovine spongiform encephalopathy to humans causing CJD (Creutzfeldt Jakob Disease)'.

No doubt fish-eaters also hope this risk is extremely low, and remains so.

Another interesting aside to the journal's report is that it confirms the potentially circular feed pattern for some meat animals.

Researchers said ground up parts of cows were fed to fish that were then fed to humans and, as pointed out previously, Sea Shepherd captain, Paul Watson, was fearful of the implications of so much ground up fish being fed to cows which were then fed to humans.

Who'd like to guess where that's all leading?

But I want to get back to Australian food standards.

If you have a moment to read them you'll notice they're written in bureaucratic language. I suppose this makes them seem thorough, efficient and effective.

I wonder how effective they really are.

Unsuccessfully I have tried to get details of how many regular meat inspections are done in Australia, what the inspections found and what was done about the findings.

I would encourage everyone concerned about the policing of Australian food standards to make their own investigations.

You may discover that government representatives, and their encasing legislation, treat corporate financial interests more seriously than public health concerns or public disclosure.

Undoubtedly the general community deserves to know how effective the system really is.

In this regard I've failed but I would love to hear from anyone who takes up the quest and has a more fruitful outcome.

和

danni
(young meat eater and zookeeper speaks)

Danni Rae sparkles as she cradles a baby wallaroo wrapped in a blanket at her breast.

You can feel the warmth Danni has for the joey she's named Heidi.

And Heidi responds.

Wide-eyed, the youngster surveys the backyard as Danni's voice and touch imprint a comforting familiarity.

Heidi and another orphaned infant, a red kangaroo named Bonnie, are being hand-raised by Danni and one of her colleagues from a small privately-owned tourist zoo in the Hunter Valley.

After two and a half years of weekend volunteer work while at high school, Danni became a full-time zookeeper at the start of 2010 and bringing little ones home to nurture just goes with the territory.

Danni grew up at Elderslie about 250 kilometres from Sydney and as a 19-year-old (11 months into a full-time job at the time of this interview) sees herself as a typical, well-adjusted Australian stepping into the adult world.

If representative, Danni sets some solid standards.

She is smart, sensitive and articulate.

A reposed confidence implies she has life on a string.

和

Danni was high school captain, finished her secondary education academically with flying colours and, at the time of this writing, spent two nights a week at college studying Captive Animal Management, certificate III.

Like most Australians she is also a meat-eater.

So I had to ask:

If you love animals how can you eat them?

'This is going to sound strange, but I think working so closely with animals actually gives me a better understanding of that question,' she said.

'Because I work with a lot of carnivores, and I feed them meat, I see that everything needs to eat.

'I come from the perspective that these predators eat meat to survive and while humans are omnivores and can eat both meat and plants, meat-eating is part of life for us.

'I grew up with it as well, mum and dad fed us meat and now it's one of those things I don't consciously think about.

'I really don't view meat as the animal it was.'

How do you feel about animals in captivity?

'I would prefer a perfect world where there were no animals in captivity.

'But in our society people want to see animals from different countries and natives that they don't usually come in contact with in their local areas.

'At the zoo we try to give our animals the best life we can in captivity, trying to enrich their lives and give them big enclosures that replicate their natural environment.'

You do love animals don't you?

'Yes, and working at the zoo is really awesome.

'It is hard work but the interaction, working side by side with the animals and having people come in and interact as well is what makes it worthwhile.

'You connect with the animals and see every one of them has their own personality and characteristics that define who they are and how they fit in as social animals or solitary animals.

'It is more than watching them, it is being part of their lives.'

What exactly do you do at the zoo?

'We clean up a lot, we pick up a lot of poo.

'There is plenty of physical work, maintaining the exhibits, raking, shovelling and then there is the tourism educational side of things.

'We do lots of shows where we feed the animals and try to get across an appreciation of the characteristics of the animals, information about their natural environment and conservation, especially about the ones in trouble in the wild.'

Such as?

'There are lots, for instance, Tasmanian devils.

和

'They're listed as endangered because their population in the wild has suffered an 80 per cent decrease because of a facial tumour disease.

'As far as I know, we are one of only two privately-owned zoos on mainland Australia with a pair that we hope to breed from to be part of the backup population for Tasmania.'

What are your favourite animals?

'I like them all but I love the dingoes (wild dogs), they're always excited to see you.

'And I love the marmosets (small squirrel-like monkeys), they only weigh 400 grams and they're so cute.'

You love them yet you eat them, is my main question too simplistic?

'Not at all, it's a fact of life, although I don't actually eat the animals I care for at the zoo.

'We eat domestic stock, cattle bred specifically for food.

'I don't think people look at a monkey for instance and think "oh, I'll be eating meat for lunch".'

As a typical Australian, do you think other people hold views similar to yours?

'Yes, I don't think most people link meat and animals.

'While I don't have a problem eating meat I understand that some people might and I respect that view but I have grown up eating it and I accept it.'

In addition to meat, you also eat eggs and dairy products, drink cows' milk and use leather products?

'Yes.'

Why?

'I don't think I've ever considered why.

'It is more a situation that I have always done it but I see it as food that's needed for people to live and grow.'

Do you think there is cruelty involved in providing these things?

'That's a hard one.

'You don't think about cruelty or animals dying.

'Meat is a package in a supermarket and I don't think about the messy side of things.

'I'm not involved in that process and when people go into a supermarket they are looking at commodities and the ethical side of things is not on their minds.'

When you go to a supermarket for meat, is the taste of it on your mind?

'That's part of the "why" question.

'Why is a simple question, but it's hard to answer.'

Which animals are okay to eat and which ones aren't okay, lets start with cows?

'I don't think there should be a difference between eating a cow or, say, a kangaroo.

'There shouldn't be a right and wrong, okay or not, even though there is an industry for cows and consumers who want the meat.

和

'When you look at it from the sense of an animal having to die for you then ethically it doesn't really seem okay but people don't link it.'

And when you're asked to link it?

'It becomes tough.'

'I'm pretty sure the animal would not want to die to feed me.'

'It sounds cruel.'

It 'sounds' cruel?

'It is cruel.'

'But from the other side, working with the carnivores in the zoo you know they have to eat to live.'

'They don't eat because they think it is okay or not, they have to live.'

And humans are animals?

'Yes.'

'We're more intelligent than other species and we're capable of looking beyond eating to live and that's when it becomes complicated.'

'I can recognise what is happening, animals are dying to become our meat and we don't really need it to survive.'

'We don't even need to eat as much as we do, but we eat it because it's available.'

So does that make it okay to eat cows and chickens, pigs, sheep, fish, you name it?

'I don't know that anyone could definitely say it was okay or not okay.'

'It's complicated.'

'I think people view meat as an easy option food, it's in the supermarket and they don't know enough about many of the alternative foods, the nutritional value of nuts for instance.'

Have you ever heard about being vegan?

'Yes.'

'Vegans are people who don't eat meat or animal products like eggs and milk.'

'Everyone is entitled to an individual perspective.'

And what about me confronting you about yours?

'I like that, it makes me think and consider what I normally don't.'

Do you think animals have feelings and a consciousness?

'I don't think they are developed to the same level as humans.'

'Obviously you can see social animals live in groups, have hierarchies and interact with each other much the same as we do even though we don't understand their noises.'

'Mother monkeys for instance look after their babies just like we do, you see the protective instincts, you can see the comparisons, so yes they have feelings and a consciousness, but it is not the same as us.'

'We have evolved further.'

Further than say a dog. Would it be okay to eat a dog?

'We're back to the okay questions.'

和

'The answer is complicated.

'People love dogs in Australia, but if I was brought up in another culture like Asia, yes it could be an accepted part of life, like eating a cow is viewed over here.'

How do you feel about using animals to test products for humans such as rubbing a facial beauty cream in the eyes of a rabbit to assess the reaction?

'That would be cruel.

'A lot of people would not buy these kind of things if they knew this was happening, but bottles on shop shelves don't have labels saying the product was tested on animals.'

Do you see a link between meat and the environment?

'If you view meat as the living animal it was then yes there is a direct link, it is a living part of its surroundings.

'But from the perspective of meat as a product then I think most people don't make that connection.'

What about meat and the health of human meat eaters?

'It works both ways, meat contains essential nutrients that benefit health, growth and survival, but over consumption can have a negative effect on these three things.

'Although nutrients found in meat can also be gained from other foods, meat is easily available and everyday Aussies know more about the nutritional value of meat than other foods.'

Thanks for the discussion Danni, how would you sum up?

'I appreciate it because it made me think about cruelty and look beyond meat as a commodity.

'All the same, I will keep eating meat because I view it as eating to live rather than an ethical thing.

"It's an accepted part of my life and although I can acknowledge that that may not be everyone's perspective it's how I view it.

'My connection with animals, like most Australians, I think is with specific animals and we're distanced enough by our culture not to change the lifestyle we accept.'

和

feelings
(one animal among many)

Do we ever consider the feelings of animals?

Do we think they could love, hate, fear, trust, experience joy, sorrow or pain like we do?

What about animals having a psychological consciousness, the ability to apply reason to situations?

Even if anyone thinks I could not produce scientific evidence to prove beyond reasonable doubt that animals have a range of feelings and emotions similar to humans, commonsense could tell us something.

Or should I say, bring a little of your instinct to bear on the situation.

A touch of clarity never goes astray.

How could the range of feelings we possess just pop up when humans came along?

How could every human possess abilities far above every other animal?

We may place ourselves at the pointy end of life's earthly spectrum but in reality we do not have a monopoly on feelings, emotions, physical sensations or consciousness.

Humans are just one creature among many, albeit a fairly arrogant one.

We have more in common with numerous species that end up on our dinner plates, are killed through our expansive habitat destruction or

和

are used as everyday 'products', than the bulk of humanity is comfortable admitting.

Uncle Mark in my family, for instance, may be as closely aligned to early anthropoidal intelligence as we've long suspected.

Jokes aside, non-human animals are not merely dumb consumer commodities.

Well they shouldn't be treated as such.

And what about our pets?

Legally they're classified in Australia as property.

We humans seem to have conveniently forgotten that other animals are sentient beings with their own powers of perception.

And a right to life.

They have a brain, a nervous system, a heartbeat and, truly, too many 'human' attributes for me to list.

Perhaps Fluffy the local butcher's pampered poodle does look strikingly like Aunty Debbie, but that's not exactly what I meant either.

Our self-importance seems to have trampled consideration of other animals.

Like Fat Controllers from *Thomas the Tank Engine* children's books, we as a species have devised a caste system of untouchable partitions and arbitrary tracks between ourselves and the rest of the animal kingdom.

I know generalisations are just that but I suspect, at this stage of our development, it's fair to say that the human race will never completely rid itself of divisions such as rich before poor, white and black, mankind and beast, native and pest, pets then animals.

Perhaps though, with sincerity of effort, we eventually could.

The very term 'animal' has widely come to mean something that does not come within cooee of humans.

The general view is that we're a sophisticated, civilised species well above life's base realm.

There are also steps within the lower echelon, for instance, a gulf between what most of us accept as a pet and what we see as an animal.

In many wealthy households pets are treated more as human than animal.

If 'animals' are considered at all they are now largely seen as wild creatures in the bush or just stock, bred as 'produce' on farms.

They are 'consumables', our future meat, eggs, wool, leather and other goods.

To my way of thinking, there is little wonder why one of our pets, for example, receives more care and protection than, say, Jenny the Jersey cow in farmer Jones' paddock or young Sally the sheep in farmer Farrington's flock.

和

Receiving something nevertheless is a lot different to deserving something.

An emotional bond builds between human family members and their pets, whereas old Jenny and little Sally may look picturesque out in the paddock but (in their breathtaking form) that's as near as they get to most people.

Out in the paddock they barely rate a second thought, let alone a first name.

When alive, they remain objects in the landscape, particularly to our ever-bulging urbanised population.

When it comes to 'product' animals, such as meat, eggs, wool and leather providers, there is scarcely any inter-species regard.

They remain black and white specks on a distant green hillside.

We humans have shielded ourselves from the brutal relationship between Jenny and a slice of succulent steak and Sally who may end her days as a lamb sandwich in a schoolchild's lunch box.

Their killing fields are behind closed doors.

The conversion of animals to meat has purposely become invisible to mainstream rich societies.

Our huge industrial slaughterhouses are comfortably locked away behind public health requirements, other legislation and commercial privacy laws.

Few people have ever seen an abattoir, let alone stepped inside one, or even contemplated working in such a place and being involved in the blood-letting.

Country people are closer than city folk to this action, but when it comes to using animals for meat, dairy products, eggs and leather goods, our society, in the main, operates on a 'what you don't see won't hurt you' principle.

There is also an overriding belief that humans have a right to 'use' animals.

It's a god-given right in many people's minds that rests on a commonly unspoken natural order.

We're conveniently conning ourselves.

Our superior race is a species set apart and if we don't look for abhorrence within abattoirs, well, it won't exist.

Right.

This veneer of 'normality' cloaks a strange savagery.

Yet I don't see the savagery strictly as a personal thing.

Individuals no longer kill to eat.

The facade is a social issue.

It is the consequence of extensive conditioning.

Centralised meat factories have moved the consequences from us to corporations and bureaucratic watchdogs.

It amounts to individual and communal denial though.

和

And the last person meat eaters want to confront them over this sort of thing is a vegan (an outsider, an extremist threatening the status quo, a ninja amongst the congregation).

The us-and-them mentality between meat eaters and non meat eaters is alive and kicking.

I have heard enough verbal lashings to testify that this divide will remain until communications from both sides markedly improve.

And that can only come from interaction.

But the passage to understanding comes not from both sides having their say as much as both sides knowing that their adversaries listened.

I accept people are generally not barbarians, lurking with murderous intent.

They don't view meat eating in these terms.

We each have our own peculiar notion of what's right, what's necessary.

We have our unique set of life circumstances and, usually, adequate interpretive and coping mechanisms to match.

In the main, people are by nature compassionate, but most simply have no genuine concept of the anguish animals endure before being killed and eaten or used as commodities.

When directly questioned about eating meat, I've found most meat eating people have no difficulty at all justifying it, even though they've usually given it very little thought.

It's one of life's necessities, repeatedly they say.

Meat simply is food.

And when asked about the treatment of animals, every single farmer I've spoken to has told me that their stock was treated humanely.

To a point I can accept what they say.

Farming men and women are largely outstanding people.

They are a genuine and generous lot in numerous respects.

They nurture their land and animals, but I feel they also apply qualifications to their world view that I can no longer apply to mine.

The livestock industry is an uncompromising system that revolves around the availability of affordable 'product'.

Its eventual underlying purpose is meat tenderness rather than tenderness of feelings toward any stock.

All farmers who grant their animals a life of minimal distress still have at least two crucial places where they look away or allow their humane reasoning to blink.

One occurs regularly as they sit down to consume a meat meal and the other is reached on each occasion their animals are carted to the saleyards.

和

These ultimate inhumanities are overlooked.

Farmers have told me that many of their decisions are hard to make.

But decisions have to be made.

People have to make a living.

And, more importantly, we have to eat to live.

As if life would cease to be without meat, they imply.

I wonder if their perceptions, or those of a major proportion of the meat eating public, would be altered if they could visit a slaughterhouse.

But slaughterhouse owners, politicians and bureaucrats use legal authority, to block public viewings.

Many years ago I had an opportunity to go into a slaughterhouse but the thought of all those raw, dead butchered beasts, hanging from metal hooks, turned my stomach and stopped me walking through the front door.

While a long way from the real thing, photographs and reports of these places and widespread industrial farming methods published in cruelty free and animal rights documents are often explicit enough to open our eyes.

They helped open mine.

I've seen too many such photographs and reports and need no further convincing.

But rather than have people recoiling from horror stories I would prefer to see positive reconciliation between humans, animals and nature as a whole.

I think life is about coexistence.

I wish it were for all humanity, like algae and fungus working together to make lichen, a compound plant living in harmony with the rocks and trees that support it.

Life is about communion.

We have to expand our vision and interact more fully with all that is around us.

But let's just stay with animals for a moment and develop the idea of being connected.

Picture Jack the pet dog and Molly the house cat.

Jack thrives on attention.

Scratch him under the ear and he'll stick by you all day.

Look into his eyes and give him a pat.

He'll give you unreserved friendship as long as his tail can wag.

Molly is different.

She can be stroppy.

At times she'll prance about and demand her space.

But soon afterwards she'll be a bundle of warmth and padded paws wanting to snuggle in.

She's one of the family.

They both are.

Now, for an instant, put that aside.

Consider what Jack and Molly would taste like.

和

Consider them as meat.

Yes, consider eating them for lunch on Sunday.

They may taste nice marinated in red wine and garlic and then roasted.

Place their plump legs or 'marbled' breast fillets on a generous sized plate with warm, mashed potato, fresh steamed broccoli and lightly boiled young, crispy carrots.

Now, imagine a moment from the dinner party.

'Mmmm, Jack is very juicy.'

'Thank you, like a sprinkle of ground pepper with him?'

'His flesh just melts in my mouth.

'Pass me a little more Molly, darling, she's so yummy.'

'She's been cooked to perfection!'

It would be an interesting dinner party.

Now, don't worry about Jack and Molly's feelings, how are you feeling?

At the risk of sounding corny, you probably find stories like that hard to swallow, hey.

They're naive.

Most likely you're revolted.

This is not positive reconciliation is it?

It's ludicrous.

Perhaps I can't avoid some objectionable stories.

In our rich Australian society, who in their right mind would actually eat Jack or Molly, even if they didn't really like pet dogs or cats?

Well, cast your thoughts back to Jenny the Jersey and Sally the sheep.

A piece of meat is more often than not only a piece of meat when you don't think about where it has come from. Or more appropriately, 'who' it has come from.

Could you consider Jenny and Sally with affection similar to Jack and Molly?

It's not as easy to care about 'things' we're detached from, is it?

Those specks on the green hillside.

Our communal perspective needs more than a little adjustment.

It is worth examining the caste system that underpins our personal and collective 'developed world' values.

How do animals fit with what our modern society actually holds store in?

I believe that for most people those specks are nothing more than dust on their footpaths.

Money, power and consumer goods largely equate to life on our brightly-lit Australian concrete pavements these days.

Well, a 'successful' life.

We're defined by our jobs and positions we hold.

Ours is very much a material world, a place where what we have speaks volumes to our contemporaries.

And ourselves.

和

In many ways, life has become a spectacle.

Multifarious advertising tantalises our senses, peeling one temptation off another.

Image, the immediate and identity matter.

There is a pace to maintain.

And the grip of established religion has slipped.

Self-control has become a quaint and awkward concept.

It's not even a ninja trait, for ninja are no longer to be found in our self-centred society, are they?

Self-control is a relic for today's 'me' generation.

Today teeters largely on technology.

A few 'lucky' people gain a podium position as envied celebrities.

But the whole developed world is propped up by sophisticated science.

Bespectacled men and women in white laboratory coats have engineered a confidence in technology that seems to provide a dazzling belief that mankind could do virtually anything.

In many minds we could remake nature itself, if need be.

For instance, grandiose, quick-fix climate change emergency schemes are being seriously researched in several countries, including America, the United Kingdom and Canada.

And bureaucrats the world over are fiddling with smaller scale techno plans.

Two of the global ideas, 'stratosphere particle injection' and 'ocean fertilising' aim to mimic nature on a grand scale to cool the planet and consume greenhouse gases.

Without doubt we could certainly improve on what comes naturally, or so overarching, science-driven, consumer theory tells us.

And who wouldn't want to believe that?

A silver bullet solution to our dullard destructiveness is so enticing.

I know humans are clever but I do not think we are more clever than nature.

Or that wise.

Human knowledge appears at times to be little more than the convenient cobbling together of arrogance, ignorance and guesstimations.

A mate of mine summed up our pretentious mentality thus: 'We worship the recycled sand our heads are buried in'.

And things, such as animals, have at best become collateral damage.

We, as a wealthy 'first world' community, have lost sight of the fundamental fact that animals, plants and the earth itself comprise the one ecosystem and each plays a part that's integral to the whole.

This ecosystem, our world, has a life force that deserves more respect than the consumable

和

glitter to which many of our society's hopes have been hitched.

Our current prosperity has drifted beyond long-term global ecological limits and delusion of our species capabilities is capped by the proposition that economics spins the globe.

Humanity has reduced itself to a race of consumers who chase the price of everything, without knowing the value of anything.

Ever expanding 'progress' is a driving impetus.

Buy, buy, buy and keep growth moving, is the mantra.

In the business world an unending push for financial profit seems harnessed to little or no respect for living communities of any sort, the environment or even its own legal constraints.

What folly to think we are more important than the very earth we stand on.

What folly to think we support nature when, in truth, it is the reverse.

What folly to think other animals are merely tucker.

Nature, all of nature, has for too long been cheaply traded as an expendable development resource.

和

beat retreat
(governmental approach to climate change)

The stupidity of what is expendable in the pursuit of 'progress' frequently stops me dead.

Onward, ever onward our species strives.

This business-as-usual myopia is a time-honoured conviction.

When push comes to shove it's out of the question to disrupt the economic status quo to deal with primary causes of diversions such as humanitarian and animal welfare issues or even global environmental concerns, no matter how looming they may be or how convincing their evident need.

Token gestures and political platitudes prevail.

In the action stakes, they're distant runners.

Here's an example.

Australian Federal Government bureaucrats have proposed abandoning extensive swathes of our continent's coast to rising seas and massive storm tides.

This 'adaptation' approach was a central principle in *Climate Change Risks to Australia's Coast*, the country's first national assessment of its type, which was made public in November 2009.

Coastal areas at risk of inundation include up to 250,000 homes plus schools, hospitals, power stations, assorted other infrastructure and numerous precious ecological places and nature communities, the report says.

和

The climate change department document was drawn up to help set national climate change coastal response priorities.

'Adaptation' was obviously cheaper (financially and politically) than other climate action such as addressing primary causes by moving Australia away from fossil fuels toward cleaner energy options, I thought.

At the same time as the risk report was tabled in Federal Parliament, the New South Wales Government Lands Minister Tony Kelly held a media briefing little more than an hour's drive from the heart of Australia's major economic hub, Sydney.

He stood at one of the Hunter Valley's vulnerable coastline spots, at Swansea, (about 70 kilometres from my home) and dismissed environmental concerns about building on such low-lying land.

Mr Kelly was confident that this state government-owned site on the ocean side of Swansea Bridge would be developed to boost regional prosperity.

So, he formally called for expressions of interest from development companies to do just that.

The national media's scant account of the risk report and coverage of Mr Kelly's coincidental up-beat announcement prompted me to closely read *Climate Change Risks to Australia's Coast*.

It begins with the words: 'Adaptation is one of the three pillars of the Australian Government's climate change strategy'.

To paraphrase the report, it says:

- A 1.1metre sea level rise was plausible by 2100, based on recent science.
- Rising sea levels will significantly change Australia's coastal zone in coming decades.
- Rising sea and climate change impacts will not stop at 2100.
- Common elements of an adaptation response, particularly for the built environment, include planned retreat, accommodating the impacts and building protective structures.
- Extreme weather events that now happen somewhere in Australia every 10 years would happen about every 10 days by 2100.
- Extreme weather events that now happen in Australia once every 100 years could be expected to occur several times a year by 2100.
- Extreme weather events are likely to be more intense, with larger and more damaging storm surge.
- Cyclones will possibly extend further south along Australia's east and west coasts.
- Strategies to retreat, accommodate or protect need to be developed as sea levels are projected to continue to rise for centuries.
- The risk report does not analyse efforts to mitigate climate change by reducing greenhouse gas pollution.
- Consultation, involving community, business and government representatives, was needed to develop a comprehensive adaptation agenda.
- Decisions need to be made on what assets to protect and how to protect them while more information was needed to ensure trade-offs and consequences were understood.

和

This national coastal risk report included brief analysis of a major storm in June 2007 that struck my region, the Hunter Valley, and adjoining Central Coast.

This 'storm event' was considered indicative of what Australia could expect at least once a year within my children's lifetime.

Once a year!

Surely not, I hoped.

It was among the biggest storms I've been in.

How will the community cope, especially as the likes of this storm have since been dwarfed by numerous other extreme weather events in Australia and overseas?

Why aren't people up in arms demanding genuine pre-emptive climate action from representatives of our various governments rather than accepting a lame business-as-usual adaptation approach like this, I thought?

But then I realised, *Climate Change Risks to Australia's Coast* was merely another government document.

Bureaucrats probably thought that by doing the report their job was done.

Media coverage came and went in a day.

Few people actually know of its existence.

Even fewer have any idea of its content.

And almost no-one cares that it is just gathering dust on some departmental shelf in a nondescript metropolitan office block along with countless other dust-catching reports.

I care though.

And I hope you also will.

The climate risk report's potted version of the June 2007 storm said that in the Hunter Valley's main city, Newcastle, 10,000 homes were flooded, 5000 cars were written off and a huge coal-carting ship was grounded on one of Newcastle's most popular surfing beaches.

The report overlooked immediate and on-going community grief the storm caused throughout the Central Coast and more than 100 kilometres up the Hunter Valley.

I was in the middle of the storm and felt its battering for 36 hours.

Our family lives on high ground at Elderslie, about 80 kilometres inland from the Newcastle foreshore.

And really, we got off very lightly at our place, mainly just having our power knocked out for a day or so and floodwaters cutting the driveway for four days.

Our family was safe and other people's property copped much worse than ours.

In Maitland, about 30 kilometres closer to Newcastle, about 4000 people were evacuated from homes for fear of water breaching a Hunter River levee bank that surrounded them.

和

Ten people died in the Hunter and Central Coast during that storm.

They included a family of four and their nephew when part of a highway collapsed plus a couple who had their vehicle swept off a bridge by a flooding river.

Remember, the climate change risk report predicted that Australians could anticipate this sort of storm 'several times a year by 2100'.

The report made three poignant points about the June 2007 storm.

- Its impact confirmed extensive flood risk modelling conducted by Newcastle City Council over several years.
- It was lucky the peak rainfall coincided with low tidal conditions so flooding and storm surge were not compounded.
- Tidal conditions one week either side of the storm would have caused far worse flooding throughout Newcastle's low-lying suburbs.

Hello.

What's going on here?

I wonder why the national coastal risk report did not even look at what could be done to reduce Australia's climate changing impacts instead of simply suggesting the nation's residents passively throw up their hands in acceptance?

Let's beat retreat.

Undoubtedly more could be done than reach for the lifeboats and call for a committee to convene and, figuratively speaking, chat about our rowing techniques.

Our society's wasteful and polluting ways have long been accelerating climate change, for heaven's sake the time has well passed for anyone to still be rooted in denial.

Trauma and destruction associated with climate change are not going to suddenly happen in some far-off decade or some far-off place and affect far-off people.

It baffled me that the risk report did not seem to immediately prod someone at some level of government to do something substantial about boosting Australia's primary pre-emptive climate change action.

Surely this report backs up uncounted prior warnings that have been twanging in our ears for too many years.

While there now appears to be a clear Australian social acceptance that we should be more liable for our lifestyle's long-term consequences there does not seem to be corresponding personal action or political will.

And that brings me back to the likes of Mr Kelly.

I believe his business-as-usual stance, and that of so many other Australian politicians, is all too typical.

和

It is so short-sightedly linked to the political re-election cycle.

To my way of thinking, it defies belief that we are now all living in a global carbon trading era, yet (if you can believe media reports) one current Australian politician in every three is still understood to be a climate change skeptic.

One in three.

Mr Kelly's announcement became a lightning rod on the issue for me.

I think Mr Kelly, as an elected community leader, you should be ashamed.

The bulk of the Australian general public no longer accept a business-as-usual stance in the face of climate change evidence.

I know, and you also should know, that many people have been calling for years for genuine, coordinated action from all leaders to reduce climate impacts.

That's what I thought.

So, before November 2009 ended, I wrote and told Mr Kelly so.

Afterward my conscience pricked.

I knew what I said could be read as a bit rude.

I know diplomacy matters, but on this occasion my short fuse won the toss and I eventually decided not to retract a word of what I said, even if I could.

Sometimes a politician's blurred vision needs a touch of bluntness to help it focus.

The situation demonstrated to me the importance of being engaged with our material world.

Accountability in politics is so often the result of public pressure.

Politicians are as human as you and me.

They can only know what common people think if we tell them.

Politicians usually interpret silence as support for their own beliefs.

So, if we rely on the judgement of other people, like Mr Kelly, we will probably get what the likes of Mr Kelly want.

If we have our say though we may get some of what we hope for.

We'll know we've had a go, and depending on the response, we'll also get a pretty good idea of what to do next.

On this occasion Mr Kelly sure did.

He went back to his Sydney office and got on with business-as-usual.

In December 2009 he was elevated to the position of New South Wales Planning Minister.

Then, three months after taking over his new political portfolio, he granted 'concept approval' for two gas or coal-fired base load electricity generators.

What about current cleaner alternatives, I thought?

和

The Hunter Valley was earmarked for one generator and the other proposed for a few hundred kilometres away, at Lithgow.

Each huge power station will have a 2000 megawatt capacity.

The business community welcomed the investment of billions of dollars and thousands of jobs the project could potentially create.

Hunter Business Chamber spokesman at the time, Peter Shinnick said that as New South Wales' electricity demand had grown by three per cent every year since 2007 both new power stations could be needed by 2015.

(That's an exaggeration, I thought, and time has proved it so.)

I could not get over the potential massive pollution and financial cost to build and then run these fossil-fuelled dinosaur power generators, so I wrote to Mr Kelly again.

I asked him to rethink his approvals, consider renewable power generation technologies, reminded him of my previous letter and again asked for a reply.

I recommended Mr Kelly investigate an Australian zero emissions economy proposal which was put forward by the community group, Beyond Zero Emissions.

To my surprise, at the end of April, 2010, Mr Kelly responded to my 2009 letter.

His 11 sentences said his government recognised global warming and had introduced 'reforms in the areas of emissions reduction and adaptation'.

The Swansea development proposal would be considered within a range of issues and should not been seen as incompatible with the government's climate change policy initiatives, Mr Kelly said.

Mr Kelly said he hoped that, subject to environmental issues being addressed, the Swansea development would deliver greater public access to the Lake Macquarie waterway, economic support and development of the local business district plus improved tourism opportunities.

Mr Kelly, you clot I thought, this is not a matter of your actions being incompatible with your own policies.

This it is a matter of your actions being incompatible with the majority view of Australians, and the scientific community which confirms humans are accelerating climate change.

The Australian community wants serious government action to reduce risk factors and help reverse human pollution impacts and the potentially devastating consequences of climate change already underway.

So I wrote to Mr Kelly a third time.

In June 2010 Mr Kelly exercised his political muscle and had the State Government block an attempt by the environmental group Greenpeace to

和

challenge plans for the proposed new Hunter and Lithgow power stations.

Mr Kelly never responded to my second or third letters and then his political party was swept out of office at the March 2011 state government election.

Sadly, the Liberal National coalition, which replaced Mr Kelly and his mates, was an even more staunch business-as-usual mob.

But before I leave the *Climate Change Risks to Australia's Coast* report I think it's worth noting that it was spotted by Lake Macquarie City Council staff.

They drew up a 'sea level rise preparedness and adoption policy' and had the potential risks added to planning certificates for 10,000 properties in the council area.

This upset a lot of people, including one of the region's biggest land subdivision developers, Jeff McCloy, who threatened legal action against the council for devaluing and restricting Lake Macquarie waterfront properties.

Mr McCloy had the last laugh when he mounted a campaign costing more than $144,000 to successfully be elected lord mayor of Newcastle in September 2012.

Coincidentally, in the same month the state government dropped its requirements for 'onerous state wide sea level rise planning benchmarks'.

Lake Macquarie City Council also fell into a more conservative line, softening its long-range planning strategy, although it maintained flooding notations on planning certificates for 10,000 properties.

Fear of waterfront properties being financially devalued spurred some residents to continue complaining about the notations.

And council representatives kept their 'adaptation' policies moving.

Late in 2013 council staff proposed 'amphibious housing' guidelines be encoded in the area's planning controls.

Such houses would be fixed to foundations on low-lying ground and 'when a flood occurs, the entire building rises up in its dock and floats there'.

In February 2014 the council approved its floating homes proposal to improve flexibility to handle floods and rising sea levels, particularly in low-lying parts of Swansea, Pelican, Blacksmiths, Marks Point, Belmont and Dora Creek.

Fantastic hey!

The well healed elite may be keen on such a Hollywood style indulgence, but it's so out of whack with what extreme climate impacts will mean for ordinary folk.

和

And before we move off politics I'd like to note that Mr Kelly became embroiled in controversy over his alleged involvement in several issues, including the state government purchase of a beach property in north Sydney and changed approval rules for a major Sydney foreshore development.

He resigned in June 2011, a couple of weeks before the government's Independent Commission Against Corruption made public a report finding he had engaged in corrupt conduct.

Mr McCloy resigned as Newcastle lord mayor in August 2014 after admitting to the corruption commission he financially donated to a couple of 2011 state election candidates.

和

dreaming
(a woman smiled as she opened the door)

The mentality of treating our primary assets as disposable is so removed from our roots that it should defy belief.

It distinctly contrasts with traditional understandings of our nation's indigenous people, the Kooris, whose ancestors are understood to have trod the Australian soil for more than 50,000 years.

Their mythological connection with nature comes from the Dreamtime, the time before time when our earth received its present form and life cycles came to be.

Spirits moved about singing, dancing, creating.

It was a profound time.

Hills and waterways sprang up, a bond between all things was engendered and when their work was done the spirits went into the sky or became animals and other earthly objects.

At birth each Koori child was given an animal totem to protect them and bestow knowledge, direction and strength throughout life.

That Dreamtime magic still holds great power for people who continue to believe, says Scott Alexander King in his book *Animal Dreaming*.

There is a primal link within nature that relates everything, the stones, trees, people, animals, everything, he says.

和

All nature comes from the one source and deserves respect.

The earth is a living, breathing entity.

She provides and teaches.

Animals have a soul.

They are part of our natural community, equal with us, and they speak to those who listen.

By respecting animals, mother earth and all her inhabitants on the same level we will ultimately learn to respect ourselves, and along the way we might just save this jewel of a planet and all her wondrous creations, Mr Alexander King says.

You can feel the energy of animals if you allow yourself.

They have a presence, like you and me.

We all have an aura.

In Chinese metaphysics this is the vital force of life—chi.

Depending on the animal, and your proximity to him or her, their distinctive air can be felt as imposing or delicate.

I cannot explain why, but for years now I have found myself drawn to the dignity of the thylacine, the Tasmanian tiger.

This striped, dog-like creature is thought to have become extinct in 1936 when the last known member of the species died in Tasmanian's Hobart Zoo, apparently of neglect.

'Benjamin' was locked out of his sheltered sleeping quarters and was exposed to a rare incident of extreme daytime heat followed by freezing night temperatures.

The fact that Benjamin was understood to be male, and only after death and better examination was found to be female, indicates how well 'he' was cared for and what we as a species know about thylacines.

Notwithstanding this, thylacines have since been 'unofficially' sighted thousands of times in bush throughout the country and now hold legendary standing like Scotland's Loch Ness monster, Tibet's abominable snowman and bunyips of Australia's mainland bush wilderness.

Tassie tigers were known to be nocturnal hunters who spent their daylight hours in caves or undergrowth.

Early sightings reported them retreating to the hills for daytime shelter, hunting small animals and birds at night and avoiding human contact.

They held endangered species status for 50 years, until 1986.

As no definitive proof of their existence had been found since Benjamin's death the International Union for Conservation of Nature officially then declared thylacines extinct.

和

The Convention on International Trade in Endangered Species of Wild Flora and Fauna has been more cautious, listing thylacines as 'possibly extinct'.

For some Australians though they did not die out.

I'm one who believes they still pad secretly on, protected by their elusiveness and the inaccessible nature of Tasmania's wilderness, such as the Weld Valley.

Thylacines are also known to have lived on mainland Australia at least 20,000 years ago, according to George Chaloupka's book *Journey in Time*.

They were companions of the Rainbow Snake, an ancestral being of indigenous Arnhem Land mythology with creative propagation powers, Mr Chaloupka said.

In Dreamtime lore the thylacine maintains a totem position of great wisdom.

Thylacine nature is about having the judgement to withdraw from the mob, walk alone for a spell and explore truths buried deep within the inner landscape, Mr King explains.

This is a time of calm to contemplate the point of our own being rather than seek outside counsel.

Thylacine thinking prompts us to stop and ask 'What is the purpose of my life? Why have I experienced all that I have?'

Study your elemental knowledge and skills, build on them and when the time is right they may be presented to the world as instruments of healing and learning, says Mr King.

Other animals, native, domesticated and exotic, have their own depth of insight that we also could draw on, he says.

Wholeheartedly I agree.

Animals have always been softly reaching out to us, if only we'd listen.

Their rustling tapers to one thing—respect.

Animals deserve better.

They have a right to life.

But that right, like all rights, should be viewed through a realistic lens.

Behave kindly to all life, rather than obsessively to anything.

To me, equality means applying a uniform approach to basic standards while trying to accept the variation of diversity.

All animals do not sit at the same table and nor would they want to.

Still, they deserve fair treatment and natural justice.

Reality dictates that no-one can live a no-impact existence so our standards are more likely to succeed if they adapt to circumstances.

And no-one should turn their personal world completely on its head in an instant, regardless of what immediately seems right or wrong.

Take a breath.

和

Reflect for a moment.

Commonsense is no more about wiping out poisonous snakes, for instance, than it is about society allowing murderers to roam our streets.

~~

Time to think is a precious commodity these days, but it is well worth the cost.

Consider matters of genuine worth to you.

Consider how all things fit together.

This is what being vegan is about.

Stop and question.

Bring practical sympathy to bear on your disposition.

Whether you can hear animals calling or think environmental security, consumer madness or something else swirls imploringly around us, there comes a time to pause our affluence.

Consider the greater good.

We need not grope for unattainable idealism though.

Something more appropriate may be nearer to hand.

I once heard a story about heaven and hell that I found helpful.

It went something like this.

A woman troubled by the decadent and debauched life she had led sought the guidance of a wise man.

'I have lost my way,' she said to the hermit.

'My confusion has reached a point where I no longer know the difference between heaven and hell.'

'Let me show you,' said he as the woman was led outside his humble abode and the world transformed.

'This is hell,' said he as they walked into a grand banquet hall.

A sumptuous feast was laid out on row after row of long wooden tables.

In came the guests.

Each carried a long metal spoon, over one metre from tip to heel.

They began to sit on long wooden benches and soon filled the hall, one line facing another across a spread of abundance.

'Only food from your spoons shall be eaten,' said the hermit to those gathered.

The woman watched as guest after guest scooped up food then spilled it as they failed to get the end into their mouths.

Soon there was much grumbling over the utensils, increasing anger at the situation generally and wasted bounty strewn about.

Within a few moments the hermit had seen enough and with resolute steps strode past the misery and waste to a side door.

The woman followed.

To her surprise, the room they entered was the same as the first, a grand banquet hall with a sumptuous feast laid out on row after row of long wooden tables.

和

'Yes, this is heaven,' said he.

In came the guests with their long metal spoons and sat facing one another across the spread of abundance.

'Only food from your spoons shall be eaten,' said he to the gathered.

The guests began like the first lot, raucously scooping, spilling and swearing.

Then some hesitated.

A thoughtful few tentatively reached out, scooped up food and gradually began manoeuvring their spoons around, offering the fare to others at the table.

Soon there was much rejoicing as all those seated realised everyone was able to partake.

The woman was smiling as she was gently shown the door with the parting words: 'Don't look back'.

和

waking
(how simple it is)

Wouldn't it be convenient if life's big decisions were as uncomplicated as heeding the words of a parable.

It would be like waking from a dream.

We would see similarities in the things that have appeared poles apart.

We would understand that reflection and some simple cooperative changes would be extremely effective aids in our travels.

We would know to smile and allow the door to click at our back as we moved forward.

The truth though is a contradiction—it is both that simple, yet that difficult.

The path, your path, mine, everyone's is not static.

There is motion in the apparently most stable of objects.

We do not have the luxury of waiting until our path is completely clear.

And few of us have a wise hermit on hand to consult before setting forth.

Again, I return to the thought that all things are part of a progression of change.

We all move whether we want to or, sometimes, even have the slightest clue about our direction.

There is also no single or unyielding guiding light.

We must step regardless.

和

However, it becomes easier if our daily choices are backed by deliberate thought within a personal framework that enables us to constructively modify our actions as circumstances allow.

A framework in harmony with creation and anchored to a breeze as it were.

For me, being vegan is as simple and as difficult as that.

It is not a destination in itself.

It is a journey of consciousness and conscience in the face of everything from the obvious to that which we can never fully comprehend.

It has helped me be more aware of my surroundings and thus apply a more measured response to commonplace reality.

It affirms my faith in humanity, its resilience and resourcefulness, despite what's obviously 'wrong' in the world and what's 'wrong' with me.

Vegan maxims as I understand them are transparent.

Vegans apply a commonsense approach to not eating meat or using animal products.

We also try to live in non-violent and practical harmony with other life, serve through education and advocacy, and strive to reduce exploitation, injustice, abuse, pollution and waste.

That's pretty highbrow, hey.

Taken to their limits these guidelines are not always possible to meet.

And they're not for everyone.

That has been one of the toughest lessons for me to accept.

Being vegan is not for everyone.

I wish it were.

But wishes don't fill dishes, and they can be confounding.

After some agonising in the year 2000 I finally admitted to myself that I had to be vegan.

While my biggest concern at the time was how the rest of my family would accept the move it was still a pretty momentous decision on a personal level.

Without a proper understanding I'd been heading to this point for a long time.

Yet in the end it didn't creep up, it just opened the pantry door one day, reached out and dragged me in.

At times, nothing is more attractive than the forbidden.

It was like that.

I couldn't say no.

It was right for that moment.

The groundwork had been done.

For decades previously there were some meats I'd been unable to stomach.

Now, they'd all be off my menu.

But I still wondered whether I could persevere forever as a dinky-di, card-carrying vegan.

和

To a degree I feared it was a hard row to hoe.

I didn't fully understand it was much more about ethics than diet.

It was one thing to have drifted generally in a particular direction and quite another to reach a conclusion where I announced to myself, and the rest of my world, a definite commitment to a specific and commonly untrodden way.

I have to try though, I told myself.

Then, once said, these words were a comfort, despite lacking a comprehensive knowledge of how to back them up.

And I kid you not when I repeat the fact—I am no cook.

Also, to my regret, as each piece of the 'how-to-survive-as-a-vegan' puzzle gradually fell into place I had an overwhelming urge to tell people.

I was damned by a need to enlighten others.

Finding balance between actively living the new me and being self-righteous was a trap.

Smugness coincided with alienation.

It was difficult maintaining good communications with family, friends and the world I occupied as, when I made the vegan decision, all secular attractions faded for me.

I now felt a mile out of kilter with what was 'right' in the eyes of those around me.

Nonetheless, it felt right for me.

This animal said to himself he no longer had to continue being animalistic to other animals, and anyone within earshot should understand ... and follow suit.

I had passed through a valley of consumer individualism and impulsive gratification to a different plane, an 'ethical', 'principled' and 'moral' place.

I was armed with such authority.

It was like arriving on the edge of a Lake Superior.

From there I had many moments 'preaching to the unconverted' and emptying myself of righteous mutterings.

Thankfully there were also moments of personal calm.

Despite my zing there were times I was able to dust the enthusiasm down with appropriate moderation.

That's when I saw that as worthy, as ethical, principled and moral my convictions may be they also carried connotations of being stodgy, spartan and, worst of all, they were socially annoying.

My doctrinal approach was creating an immediate turn-off and not just for the uninitiated.

Negative reactions were the consequence of my pushiness.

Little by little though I realised good intentions were no excuse for tofu tub-thumping, or any other form of tub-thumping for that matter.

和

Eventually I saw I'd been a fool, drumming out dogma so (thankfully) I pulled my head in.

It's strange though, I've personally never considered veganism as a restrictive or suffocating condition governed by the tightest of rules.

In some ways it has felt like an acrobat's safety net.

In my head I knew it was a way to live, rather than a fixed end position, yet here I was in my dogma moments defining rather than living.

Luckily my initial optimism grew stronger and stronger.

I grasped that living did not have to include eulogising.

No, I couldn't eat all sorts of stuff, couldn't buy leather items or products tested on animals, but there were many more positive things I could do.

Veganism really came to me as a breath of fresh air.

It tapped as contentedly as rain on a tin roof.

In the years leading towards my decision I had been modifying a routine here, planting an occasional seed there, changing some habits and making little alterations where I could.

The progression went largely unnoticed up to a time when another seemingly simple adjustment became a tipping point.

The horizon had become solid ground, a region in deep accord with nature which could be sustained by compassionate and clear daily choice.

It was no longer a conceptual vista a long way off.

It was here and this was the time.

It was time to unfasten the final constraints.

It would be okay from here on to say: 'Sorry, I don't eat animals or use animal products'.

It would be okay not to fit in the 'normal' mould, especially if I was considerate rather than self-centred.

It was okay to be part of what others saw as a fanatical group.

At that moment I wasn't concerned about what I would eat, as long as it was not meat.

Doing my small bit each day to lower the livestock industry's impacts, continuing to improve our environment generally and reduce animal suffering were foremost in my thinking.

The personal health benefits of being vegan were a bonus.

There was no compelling requirement to throw out everything that had been tainted by the pain of animals and blood of the environment.

Using what was already at hand and recycling made more sense than buying in a load of new stuff, I thought.

There was a need to learn.

There was also a good dose of uncertainty to deal with.

'Could I really live in practical harmony?'

和

'Would I sink or swim beyond my conventional comfort zone?'

Then several days after the decision I began to feel incredibly light.

If you ask Julie and our children they would probably say I'd merely returned to a usual state of light-headedness.

In fact it was a physical and mental lightness that has stayed with me.

There was a release, a weight lifted and scariness of the unknown receded.

I can only explain it as a freshened frame of mind, a certain clarity of intent, coupled with revived physical energy.

As days turned to weeks, months then years I was never seriously bitten by the vegan cooking bug, instead I became intrigued by the vegan matrix, the Tao as it were, of how being vegan intersected the practical, spiritual, philosophical and my understanding of faith.

So now I'm convinced that being vegan is an emerging global religion.

That said, I'd like to offer what follows as an explanation rather than an exercise in evangelism.

Firstly, anyone who associates being vegan with an obsessive diet has missed the elephant in the room.

I see it as stepping aside from the rigid mainstream regime of killing and abusing animals for our eating and consumer enjoyment.

That's obsessive.

While what vegans eat or don't is of daily importance, that aspect is a consequence of applied reason.

Food is a major focus, but not the only focus.

Living is the focus, living a particular way as parents, children, lovers, workers, ninja or whatever we are.

I see veganism as offering hope and meaning.

With these, we're free.

They have strengthened my trust in life.

And my flexibility, in several ways, has picked up.

I can't say that gentleness is a strategic guarantee to inherit the earth, but it may well be.

It's certainly preferable to destructive and wasteful alternatives.

Being vegan has made it obvious that having 'everything' is within reach.

Just as I have moved away from animal slaughter I understand that bucket loads of more money are not the answer to life's central questions.

I just have to want less of the superficial.

We all could recognise what we already have.

No-one needs half the stuff the material world propagandists want us to chase.

Caring for all life and the planet itself, appreciating what surrounds us, setting realistic goals and living within financial and physical means are not

和

an existence of deprivation.

They're attainable, satisfying and in fact uplifting.

Being vegan can stand alone as a way to give life purpose.

It can also overlay your life without requiring all past religious experience or secular baggage to be jettisoned.

This is where it fits in for me, extending, complimenting and replacing some traditions I grew up with.

Being born into a meat eating family predisposed me to a life that clung tightly for decades.

Though now there are aspects that I choose, and choose not, to embrace.

I was Catholic before I was vegan, but now I view things the other way round.

I see through vegan eyes before, but not to the exclusion of, other perspectives.

For me this helps with the blending of life experiences.

It simply is what is.

It uncomplicates.

The reasons behind what each of us do nevertheless are complex.

Who amongst us fully understand themselves?

I don't wake each morning for instance and think: 'Wow, I'm a vegan today.'

I don't intentionally go around each morning categorising myself, anyone or anything else for that matter.

I simply live, and try to live simply.

Being vegan is now just absorbed into my acceptance, although that sounds too pretentious to be accurate because I live and breathe a fairly unromantic and uneventful life.

It's not as though I come home at the end of a working day and squat down with other dark clad ninja figures to secretly plot the downfall of some evil, capitalistic corporation that abuses animals and mercilessly pollutes our world.

(Not every night, hey!).

In an ordinary way I am interested in enriching my time on earth, raising my eyes to scan the distance and take surer steps, but those steps are genuinely very much commonplace.

And while I maintain a healthy urge to compete I now have a firm feeling of 'being' mixed in with my striving.

I find veganism is a strong directional sliver on a subconscious plane, a clear reference, calmly coexisting with the mundane and high points alike.

By that I mean it is one of the decisive things that help me believe in whatever I do without a need to put on an obvious or outward show for others.

It helps keep me in touch with both the eternal and the here-and-now while still allowing me to

和

comfortably partake in choice.

Some traditional religious ritual, for instance, retains great value for me.

It also helps provide a positive structure for huge numbers of people and thus is familiar and accessible ground for many notable community contributions.

Where appropriate, I see some ritual as a universal language that helps people reach inner feelings, connect with each other and share experiences 'normal' to us all.

Singing and rhythmic chants can enliven everyone.

As I consider it further, I suppose I should be reluctant to call veganism a religion.

It has no cloistered church or patrolling clerics.

It lacks an extent of definition that comes with the historic existence of traditional religions.

Okay, it's embryonic.

So why categorise it thus anyway, after all religion is the domain of paedophile priests, gullible happy clappers, fundamental extremists and banal televangelists.

The consequences of stereotyped offensive aspects of established religions seem, in certain quarters, to grow by the minute.

To a degree, it appears that some traditional religion, although having many solid foundation principles, has degenerated into a cult, based on blind faith that fails to properly act on immoral and corrupt behaviour in a vain hope of protecting the institution's public reputation.

Add crusading devout and social do-gooders to the assembly and you have a real mix of excess.

No wonder traditional religion is waning in my part of the world, and other developed countries.

There's no doubt about its shortcomings, but that's far from a complete picture and it's a pity the vast majority of good people of every religious following and their honourable works have, at times, been cloaked by a misguided and violating minority.

Vegans are similar.

In some mainstream quarters they have been stigmatised, not in quite the same manner as some religious types, but stereotyped all the same as rabblerousing radicals, sanctimonious and extreme in their thinking, living habits, and particularly their diets.

In some cases the criticisms are warranted.

Although, vegans actually comprise a cross-section of society with a majority being good and honourable and only a tiny element could genuinely be labelled as extreme in any sense.

While I believe veganism holds substance on a multitude of levels, as a group, vegans are just as prone to human frailties as any other collective.

和

No-one is beyond reproach.

No-one is beyond change either.

And that includes the sanctimonious.

Even extremists, no matter where they may be, are as entitled to the same basic fair treatment that you and I personally hope for.

As I've said before, that boils down to respect.

I see being vegan as a new religion because the concept is an ideal—to live in peace and harmony with all creation.

Like any ideal, it's a target in motion.

It incorporates elements such as a broad consciousness of the sacred nature of life, reason to face our own prejudices, acknowledgement of a 'god' or universal force, the value of useful activity and examination of the world's underlying principles.

It encourages continued mindful questioning, restores a connection and faith in our earthly ecosystem, provides a platform for personal conduct and consideration of others which is a levelling factor and, most of all, awareness of our own insecurities in which lies the answer to our fears.

I believe religion should mainly be about spiritual application.

It should centre on guiding, listening and responding rather than controlling and judging.

To me, religion is akin to tai chi, the meditative oriental exercises at the root of martial arts.

From a religious perspective, veganism is just that, a moving meditation within a world view.

It is the daily demonstration of gradual personal improvement, regardless of whether or not a vegan is widely considered part of a real church— or even a devious ninja.

Being vegan allows those involved to gauge and express their worth in a more down-to-earth way, rather than through a traditionally religious or shallow, materialist fashion.

It is about taking an active 'thou shall', rather than 'thou shall not', approach to life.

It helps me focus on self-awareness; empathy with people, other animals and nature; the need for contemplation, discipline and perseverance; forgiveness of others and myself; humour in the face of disappointment; tolerance of seemingly unpardonable circumstances; and confidence to make an effort.

It is a sense of calm.

Aligning with any 'religion', or simply attending any church though does not make anyone religious, any more than standing in a garage would make them a car.

That's something one of my daughters once said and she assures me she is usually right.

Who am I to argue?

和

For years I was nagged by a need to be 'right'.

I'm not as irritated by that need these days but, like an alcoholic, I attempt to be mindful of my limitations.

And I ask myself: 'Are we not all a mixture of compassion and anger?'

和

child by a well
(an existence that ripples)

Every one of us can be deflated at times by our imperfections and the restrictions of circumstance.

Some people perpetually bear their degree of misery without realising they are actually living like a fabled water bearer.

You may have heard a version of the tale.

A water bearer went each day to a well a long distance from his home.

He only had a cracked earthen jar to collect water for drinking, cooking and washing.

When he returned to his wife and children the jar was always partly empty.

Occasionally the family struggled to get by on what was provided.

The water bearer was unable to stop the leak and felt unworthy of the graces and responsibilities life had granted him.

Then one day he met a child resting by the well.

The child was waiting to thank him.

Every time the water bearer had filled his cracked jar and trudged homeward with it swinging at the end of a wooden pole he held on his shoulder, some of what leaked out had watered grass and flowers along the track.

The child had watched the water bearer and picked the grass to feed animals at home while the flowers became precious gifts for his ailing mother.

和

The child's mother had asked him to say 'thank you' as the flowers had brought rare moments of joy to her deathbed.

The realisation of his unknown gift engulfed the water bearer.

It unfastened his burden of guilt and lifted a veil which had shrouded his pedestrian existence.

In a similar way, I discovered the vegan perspective loosened burdens I was not fully aware of and it gently watered my perception of relationships with other people, animals, nature and our man-made world.

It gave me a cloudless picture of my proportion, where I sat in the natural order.

It made it easier to see and ultimately accept my good and bad points and what life expected of me.

It also helped me realise that no-one could fully understand the ripples of this existence, regardless of it being obviously pedestrian or exemplary.

Whether we bear burdens of unworthiness, self-importance, guilt or anything else we all seem to carry weight of some kind that can be hard to dislodge.

These burdens are a spiritual gravity that can add to our daily inertia.

Many people either don't recognise their rootedness or have not reached a point of desire to examine it.

For others there is an urgent personal questioning that resonates within their souls.

Without discrimination it can touch men, women and children from the highest stations through to outcasts such as drug addicts and criminals in jail.

The questioning comes in many ways.

Eventually it is a reassessment of life's meaning.

It is a search for life's missing piece.

A search for our missing peace.

Often the quest begins with the realisation of a subliminal truth, 'something' is not quite right.

Our time on this earth is limited and 'something' needs attending to.

There is a rap on the windowpane of conscience and it won't go away until we attend to it.

It can also feel like fading.

We fade like all else before our eyes and as the grey increases we can feel pressed to ask what have we done with our limited personal resources?

What have we done for the wider good?

Will we be lucky enough to contentedly rustle among life's autumn leaves?

What legacy will we be part of?

Often as we fade the question arises: 'Does it really matter how our time plays out?'

Yes, I believe it sure does.

和

The connectedness we feel between all living things, and the earth itself, extends from the actions of our ancestors to future generations.

~~

I've found that being vegan has provided me with an unmistakable god consciousness, a tangible depth to plumb for all sorts of queries.

Regard for nature, life in its kaleidoscope of variables, and respect for yourself are aspects of a god consciousness.

This sensibility recognises that god is within you and me and at the same time all that surrounds us, regardless of what name god goes by.

The word god though is so clumsy, and descriptively inaccurate.

Veganism does not have its own god, like Jesus Christ, Allah, Krishna, Buddha or Jehovah from the traditional religions.

Veganism is prayerful though and definitely a path which recognises god.

Without a god could a pile of lifeless chemicals combine to form living matter that could reproduce itself?

For life to begin, gain equilibrium and continue it's rebirthing and ascending cycles there is something here that's beyond our comprehension, a god, a universal creator or indescribable essence that is the heartbeat of reality.

I am not necessarily talking about a human-like image or a being with super-duper or infallible powers.

God is visualised in many forms and even as something with no form at all by some people.

The term 'god' is humanity's best effort to define a complicated concept that truly we can't get hold of.

Questioning who, or what, is god comes down to boundaries.

We put boundaries around 'him' to contain what we can't understand or prove, because we can't bear not knowing or not having an answer.

Even scientists, those men and women who live and breathe 'fact', can't escape using the word god.

For example, in July 2012, world-leading nuclear physicists announced a breakthrough in a $10billion experiment to prove an idea one of them theorised in the 1960s, the force believed to give matter its mass, a basic building block of the universe.

And what did they say they thought they'd found— 'the god particle'.

I grew up knowing god as 'three people in one', a black-bearded Jesus Christ on earth, his grey-bearded father floating in the clouds above and their uniting spiritual aspect, 'the holy ghost'.

和

I still see god in these terms on occasions, but I am more often consoled by a latter day thought that god is an unfathomable that is both the chaos and order of life.

If it is easier to understand and visualise god as an enlightened being who walked the earth with other humans, that's fine.

These days I feel god differently.

God is a universal entity for me, the misty mechanics that mesh together material things and the ethereal realm of angels from which it seems our earthly prayers are sometimes answered.

My uncouth words cannot reach the abstract.

The morality and reasoning that comprise god easily slip through my fingers.

I feel god in things such as the mystique of reproductive power in a seed, the soft beauty of a butterfly, the scent of rain, penetrating tranquillity among trees and the smile in a stranger's eyes.

Being vegan is about re-attaching to that essence, touching its presence through a practical respect for life.

It is about acknowledging rather than having a definitive understanding, or an answer for everything.

It is tasting our personal humility and being engaged with the vastness that encompasses us.

Being vegan is recognition that we are not separate from nature, nor should we feel superior to any piece of nature in a wanton or wasteful way.

If we think we are superior to someone or something, shouldn't we help them?

We are fragments in a life force, not independent but interdependent.

After years of reaching I can now get hold of the idea that it is futile to think of ourselves as separate individuals.

There really is no such thing as 'self', no independent self.

We are what we are only because of the other people, other life, circumstances, knowledge and the immaterial and material objects around us.

We are here to interact with our environment through an expanding sympathetic consciousness.

Being vegan comes down to a physical application within this concept, considering our choices and attempting to employ them.

It is about accepting that while the world is not always equal, fair or just from our confined perspective we are still somehow obliged to do our bit for equality, fairness and justice within our concept of the natural order.

Our particular harmony gathers meaning through practice.

Practice aligns personal values and deeds.

和

And to my way of thinking that is the biggest attraction to being vegan, the way aspiring to be one with life's natural rhythms can be felt and expressed at such a deep and intimate level.

It is being as aware as possible of the here and now, trying to improve things in all we do rather than just minimise our negativities.

The prayerful aspect of being vegan really is the same as thoughtfulness in general or prayerfulness in other religions.

It is simply the manner in which people conduct their ordinary lives, if our daily practice buds with right intent we're mindful of listening to others, regularly reassess and endure with respect.

To me this is the substance of living prayer.

It includes inner communication, trying to silence the world's constant noise and stilling the chatter in our heads from time to time so we can find guidance in our own personal way without continually calling on an almighty power to step in and take away our responsibilities.

And a prayerful life does not have to exclude secular rewards such as money and notoriety.

It calls for a balance between how much we 'need' and what we do with our needs.

Some vegans may be outspoken in spite of the attention they draw.

Judgemental people may view someone confidently standing up for their convictions as a self-interest seeker.

A genuine prayerful person though will strive to understand their own primary motivations and this helps them both understand other people and the broader community understand them.

As individuals we make a difference, directly and indirectly.

As an increasing number of vegan individuals we can make an increasing collective difference greater than just adding all our personal efforts together.

I've pondered long and hard about my vegan thoughts and actions and come to the conclusion that they are not weird, as some critics may suggest.

They may not always line up with mainstream expectations, for sure.

They are not even radical.

They are just ordinary truths, truths that make sense to the likes of me.

和

searching
souls
(alone we aren't)

More people appear to be soul searching these days.

They are less anesthetized by consumerism's hazy fluorescent glare.

Push-button promises and fleshy pursuits are providing them the barest satisfaction.

Their personal dimensions are requiring more honest and relevant attention as they seek to define 'true self'.

They want less formality in their lives.

They are moving away from dictatorial frameworks, and their often dubious authoritarian advocates, towards meaningful two-way dialogue with the world.

And they also want a greater say on a wider social level.

Accepted, there's always been a degree of searching.

Perhaps I'm simply more aware of it at present because I'm here now.

I'm reminded of a billboard sign I was once told of out the front of a church in the Sydney suburb of Manly some years back.

It asked: 'What would you do if God came to Manly today?'

Using an indelible black marker pen, someone is said to have written on the sign: 'I'd move Branighan to the wing and Fulton to half-back.'

This exchange speaks volumes to me about social trends and trying to be engaged.

和

It tells of a person in traditional religion reaching through their cloistered confines and someone outside connecting by saying yes, there is a place for god in secular society.

We could even find him a spot in a reshuffled local football team.

Billboards are a rudimentary forerunning form of today's mass media.

And for all its faults, the media industry of television, computer and smart phone-based internet connections, radio, newspapers and so on has brought a more expansive and almost instantaneous global understanding to humanity.

Despite the confusion engendered by consumerism's continual bombardment, I believe media on the whole, has also sparked an increased longing for purpose in our collective consciousness.

I know that far from always seems apparent amid the all too regular inane media pap.

And while the majority in our rich society may not yet be convinced, it seems to me that a growing broad mix of people are trying to do something about pervasive consumption and its destructive consequences.

There is a desire to be a more worthwhile part of our herd and contribute to its overall wellbeing.

Consciousness is affecting people by increments.

The most acute example of this is public awareness of our deteriorating global environment and humanity's accelerating contribution.

Until recently the enormity and complexity of the situation has largely resulted in the livestock industry's environmental impacts being ignored.

Today though, it does face a degree of opposition.

The climate change debate has also strengthened the resolve of some common individuals keen to do something about their concerns, regardless of their modest means to address it.

While coming from all walks of life, these people are alike in their attempts to ground their thinking, clarify worthwhile priorities and share more as they venture toward their own truths.

A growing number are uniting a need for extensive environmental action with their day to day activities.

These people are watching, listening, being intuitive and incorporating ideas of value to themselves from diverse arenas.

I see this approach as the crux of success for us personally, and as a global species.

We are like trees.

Our long-term survival depends on living as part of a forest, working together and drawing on our collective power as much as our individual strengths.

和

While a ninja for instance has distinct skills, teamwork is often essential for their success.

I see it as crucial that humans of all persuasions interact with as diverse a range of people as we are able so as to better perceive which aspects of our understanding are worth holding and which may be weeded.

It is important we keep learning, searching for answers, adapting and seeking meaningful compromise.

Compromise can be difficult, but it can also help build a workable foundation for achievement.

I'm not advocating anyone becomes a conformist or forgoes their core principles to comply with traditional expectations, such as a vegan intentionally eating meat on occasions to 'fit in'.

Compromise is driven by examining our tendency to judge rather than reconcile.

For instance, at the start of my vegan years I found it hard to draw a distinction between a dislike of meat eating and a dislike of meat eaters.

I've since seen that none of us are the sum total of one, or even several attributes.

My 'right and wrong' type of thinking, particularly in the early days, was ingrained.

I now try to accept meat eaters still eating meat by acknowledging that all meat eaters have a worth well beyond what I view as a glaring flaw.

Hopefully they too can look past my conspicuous flaws.

I would do well to remember that in life it is the search for truth and purpose that matters, not in whose name the search is conducted.

Who amongst us is not in some way conflicted?

Again, I'm reminded, while being vegan may hold many answers it does not hold them all.

It adds another layer to my thinking that sieves out clutter and acts like a brace to reinforce my actions but is not a sturdy staff to permanently prevent me, or anyone, from failing at times to make sense of the world.

There may be good reasons for certain things happening, but sometimes those good reasons are well and truly beyond me.

I suppose a central point I gather from being vegan is that life is not about dwelling in an unending perfect peace.

It is often about finding joy in our humble and ordinary activities, facing what presents itself, learning from trials and triumphs and attempting to contact and continue to reclaim an inner peace as we strive to survive along with all forms of life.

Yes, we must work cooperatively with people of every peculiar persuasion and we must also work on a balance that includes saying 'no' when we reach a line that bounds our principles.

和

Times when difficult decisions must be made are when we should look into our hearts for a way forward as a compassionate path leads away from conflict.

And that is easier said than done.

It can take some time before my stubbornness looks away from conflict and I can say to myself: 'Okay, we have a problem. What can I actually do to help sort it out?'

A genuine desire to sort something out is the key factor.

Once I reach that point it is easier to see that underneath any turmoil headed for reasonable resolution lies a desire for peace, on both sides of the argument.

Tolerance can then surface and compromise becomes possible.

In our household, for instance, I have tried to back off sermonising in support of the animal kingdom, opposition to corporate greed and frustration with communal environmental ignorance.

Now tension levels have dropped, family members and friends from far afield have tried to accommodate my veganism and gone out of their way to make vegan dishes for various functions and everyday meals.

I am happier today to see carnivores in my circle reducing their meat intake and being more aware of animal cruelty and the link between the livestock industry, personal health and environmental degradation.

While I don't condone slaughtering and eating animals, or the planet's destruction, I now try to focus my action rather than take a scattergun approach trying to hit every target.

Sure, this is a fairly small step in the grand scheme of things, but it is a cooperative step not a begrudging one and I don't believe it to be isolated.

I know there is no reason why anyone couldn't become a vegan immediately without a transition, but I would rather acknowledge the movement that anyone makes in that direction than continually scowl at what remains to be done.

I've tried making vegan family meals and must admit it is very pleasing to have people hoe in and then pass me a compliment.

Perhaps I could become 'a real cook' after all, I kid myself.

But next time I'm working my way through a recipe, searching for ingredients or bemoaning how long things take, I have a revised perspective.

Cooking just doesn't come easy to me.

I need to keep working at it.

That's a safer thought.

Whether other people view veganism as an emerging religion or not doesn't really matter.

和

I know that without a promise of eternal life, earthly fame or financial fortune, being vegan can still provide a sense of purposeful attachment throughout our shifting life cycles.

It affords me the drive to power my actions and calm to accept downtime in this imperfect and demanding world.

Being vegan is not a perpetual march in serious, non-leather boots.

It also encompasses growth through play, laughter, love, moments in the sunshine, gardening and exercise.

It includes our own pleasurable time in the park.

And that reminds me of George Best.

He was an Irish-born lad who grew into a soccer playing genius in the highest European league during the 1960s and '70s.

He was magical to watch and became one of the world's first footballers to make millions—and spend it all.

Later in life he was asked: 'Where did it all go?'

He answered thus: 'I spent a lot of money on booze, birds and fast cars.'

'The rest, I just squandered.'

Life's like that—it's about perspective.

和

velocipede
(guardian spirits and bikes)

It's a great word, isn't it?

When I first heard 'velocipede' I thought it must be the name of a beautiful nocturnal creature, sort of like a gecko.

In my mind this animal had an ancient origin.

It was compact, about 30 centimetres long, adaptive, shy and mobile on four thin, muscular legs.

Its tactile paws padded the earth softly and enabled it to nimbly climb and attach in any terrain.

I could see velocipedes draped in muted tones of green, grey and light brown.

They were subtle yet colourful, camouflaged joys to behold.

These rare reptiles lived in bushland seclusion while keeping a silent eye on humans and our boisterous behaviour.

Guardian spirits I took them to be.

Some people may think this kind of animal remains a figment of my imagination.

Perhaps, but I believe guardians exist.

Some people know them as angels.

I can't explain them any more than to say I've felt their guiding and protection in times of need.

和

And I accept, they're not called velocipedes.

The word velocipede actually comes from Latin.

It originally meant swift foot, but has evolved into the collective term for a human-powered vehicle with one wheel or more.

Today's most common velocipede is the bicycle.

The earliest version is understood to have been made of wood and built in Germany in 1817.

The word velocipede came into use in the 1860s with the development in France of a 'boneshaker'.

It was also made of wood, with later models having metal tyres.

Global advances in metallurgy during the 1870s led to the first metal frame velocipedes.

Pedals were attached to the front wheel and as the machine was further updated the front wheel became larger and received solid rubber tyres.

These 'penny-farthings' were the first velocipedes to be called bicycles.

Current bikes are technically a world apart from the originals, being much more useful, safer and comfortable.

They're a neat fit with a vegan life.

To me they're virtually a vegan utensil.

They are environmentally harmonious and positively interactive for users.

I love bikes.

I see them as a universal piece of equipment essential to sustaining our species and thus reducing our impact on other species and our world.

Although every person on earth does not have to ride them, I believe bikes must play an on-going major role if civilisation is to seriously reduce its planetary destruction.

Bikes are also extremely advantageous in our personal lives.

Humans, like all animals, must be active.

Now I'm at a point in life where the older I get the better I was and extreme sports are no longer on my must-do radar, I try to do things appropriate for my circumstances.

We all should.

Outside a few sneaky ninja things (such as a spot of guerrilla gardening) my main recreational fresh air fix largely comes from walking, practicing tai chi and riding a bike.

Bikes have been part of my life since tiny tot days.

Well, my first velocipede was actually a trike, a beaut little red three-wheeler.

As a very young child I ran away from home on that machine.

At the time, my younger brother Waide had a bright blue pedal-car made of pressed tin.

Without telling anyone, one day we decided to visit our grandmother and just pedalled off.

He was four and I was five.

和

Soon, our parents realised we had disappeared and before long had the police and half the neighbourhood out searching.

That sturdy trike and Waide's pedal-car eventually carried us several kilometres (even across the New England Highway) to grandmas, but that's another story.

It is also an adventure that I think subconsciously established my link between bikes and escape.

Bikes have provided me with plenty of play, laughter, time in the sun, alternative transport and, of course, physical exercise.

Rain or shine these days I feel a sense of glee while pushing bike pedals east down the highway past gridlocked motor vehicles creeping west in the peak hour dawn gloom for another shift at the region's coalmines.

Sometimes as I spin through suburbia on my mountain bike I feel a twinge of sorrow for the latest crop of children whose lifestyles are more attuned to electronic entertainment devices, television, mobile phones, earplug music systems and the convenience of 'fast food' shops on so many street corners.

The value of getting out and about, whether on a bike, aimlessly kicking a football or just mucking around in a park diminished in carefree Australia during the years that transported me to adulthood.

Don't misunderstand, I know there are stacks of young and old people who still regularly do plenty of sport and outdoor activity.

But, on the whole, affluent human populations worldwide have an obesity epidemic that is expanding by the day.

And a lack of outdoor activity is a direct contributor.

Newcastle University associate professor David Lubans says the prevalence of obesity has trebled in the past 30 years, with one in every four Australian youngsters either overweight or obese.

Fat kids face a range of adverse health issues and obese children are likely to become obese adults with an even broader range of health problems.

More than a reasonable slurp of 'soft' drinks and 'energy' drinks and excessive time in front of electronic screens are also high among the weight gain culprits, particularly for teenage boys.

It's strange this addiction to switch on the outside world yet fear turning it off.

Additionally, an underlying communal anxiety seems to have taken hold these days so that children do not wander as freely as in my youth.

They are generally more supervised and likely to be chauffeured to and from school, whereas I cannot recall a single day when I did not either walk or ride to school. (No doubt though, my parents did take me on occasions but they're too rare to remember.)

和

When I was little I walked with the kids across the street and as I grew I gained my own to and from school entourage.

Thankfully, the playtime of my adolescence has only faded within some sections of our society and not completely evaporated.

As youngsters we didn't spend so much time outside because we were intrinsically better than today's kids or had any greater knowledge of its benefits.

We simply didn't have the same options.

Many of today's electronic gizmos for instance were little more than science fiction or black and white drawings in *Dick Tracy* newspaper comics when I was growing up.

Only now, with five adult children, do I see regular exercise as one of the seven invigorating elements of a fortunate life for our whole community along with spiritual growth, love, a healthy diet, community participation, work and rest.

In fact, it's through rest that we gain the benefits of exercise and active interaction with our world.

It allows our muscles to absorb our exertion, recuperate and prepare for more.

A fortunate life is just that, not something we entirely create or control.

It's not predestined, regardless of what we do or think. It involves our choices, luck and other influences which are guided by powers beyond us.

A fortunate life hinges on attitude—our willingness to recognise how fortunate we really are and make the most of what we have.

There is an old American Indian saying that goes like this:

'Give thanks for the morning light,
thanks for your strength,
thanks for your food,
and thanks for the joy of living.
If you see no reason for thanks, look within.'

But again I digress.

Ah yes, bikes.

If I had to boil my world view down to a few basic words they would be something like this: 'Give up meat and get a bike.'

Bikes have long been my exercise option of choice, although I see them as much more than an exercise apparatus.

They're a most efficient and practical conveyance.

They're pollution fighters.

And they're toys that help me feel alive and physically grateful for my fortunate life.

On a bike I become a child again as I bump down our driveway to the front gate and zoom over the little hump left by car wheel tracks in the gravel.

I can bounce onto the bitumen stretching east-west past our home without a care in the world.

Everytime.

和

It's the fun aspect of cycling that keeps me at it (even though I'm less often in the saddle than I'd like to be).

Despite bike use by Australian children and teenagers dropping in my lifetime, they all haven't given it away and more bikes, overall, are now consistently sold every year in the country than cars because adults are returning to them in an effort to hold onto more than youthful memories.

Thankfully regular riders have come to terms with their self-consciousness and fear of being hurt to embrace these wonderful contraptions.

Richard Ballantine draws great imagery in his book *Richard's Bicycle Book* when he says that bikes are just as important as Mrs Grundy's spinach.

Unquestionably good for you.

I'd like to see both bikes and spinach commonplace in every home.

Richard points out that a bike will pay for itself, is often quicker in cities than a car and with the regular exercise they accommodate you can expect to live longer, think better and be more resistant to injury.

One of the biggest benefits of bike riding is that it exposes the rider to sunlight.

The sun's ultraviolet rays help our skin produce vitamin D.

Vitamin D allows us to absorb calcium into our bloodstream from the food in our intestines, according to doctor Michael Klaper in his book *Vegan Nutrition: Pure and Simple.*

Vitamin D plays a part in an amazing number of bodily functions that help ward off disease associated with heart attacks and strokes, increase bone strength and reduce high blood pressure.

It is also good for our immune, respiratory and reproductive systems plus food digestion and weight management.

Boston professor and vitamin expert, Michael Holick, says vitamin D deficiency increases risks for pregnant women, plus heart disease, type two diabetes and infectious diseases.

Not only is sunlight the ideal way to get vitamin D, according to New South Wales Natural Health Society spokesman Roger French, our bodies self-regulate the amount we receive.

He says studies have shown that between 20 minutes and two hours in the sun daily, depending on skin type and environmental factors, should naturally optimise our vitamin D levels.

Regular sun exposure, while avoiding sunburn, makes sense whether you are vegan or not.

It decreases the risk of numerous common human cancers, including the skin cancer melanoma.

和

It is significant that melanoma is more prevalent for indoor workers than outdoor workers and also more common on parts of our bodies not exposed to the sun, Mr French says.

The real cause of rising melanoma rates is at least partly due to a reduction in people's vitamin D, he says.

Now before we go further into health and nutritional matters I want to make it clear that my 'formal qualifications' in this field are on par with my formal cooking credentials—nil.

But hopefully I've learned a little more than nil in my earthly travels.

As a commoner I largely rely on the commonsense of life's lessons and that includes seeking wise counsel and appropriate reading materials where necessary. Just as you need not write a university postgraduate thesis on *Nanoparticles for Bulk-Hetrojunctional Solar Cells* to run your home on either stand-alone or grid-linked renewable power you don't need anywhere near uni, or any other tertiary college education qualifications in nutrition to be healthy—whether you're vegan or not.

Commonsense is a valuable resource.

Most forms of life rely on it.

It freely passes from every generation to the next.

It's not hard to pick up enough nutritional basics to ensure we thrive on a fantastically tasty and healthy vegan diet.

The main thing is diversity.

It should be balanced and comprise a wide variety of foods.

As a thumbnail suggestion I'd say a great vegan diet should include such things as plenty of green and leafy vegetables, (broccoli, beans, spinach and lettuce), coloured foods including carrots, tomatoes and beetroot, plus vegetable oils, cereals, grains, nuts, seeds and fruit, the best being freshly picked, organic and local if possible.

The plant kingdom has plenty of diversity to suit everyone's desires.

And things such as tofu, soy and pastry products add to the treat.

Pay attention to the way you and other people eat, work, rest and play.

Don't shy away from asking questions about your concerns and always expand your knowledge.

See a professional quickly if you have any specific health or medical issues.

Enjoy life and don't dwell in fear as a fear confronted is rarely as scary as anything left unchallenged.

I find many people within the meat eating fraternity to be oddly fearful of vegans.

More precisely, they seem more fearful of what vegans do and don't eat—as if we were the ones on a poisonous diet.

I'm not sure whether their underlying apprehension

和

is about their own welfare, the vegan's or they're simply trying to make some canny point-scoring carnivore comment.

They ask questions like:

'Where do you get your protein?'

'What about iron, or calcium?'

'And what about things like Omega 3 and vitamins?'

These are the type of self-doubt questions that can stump people in the early stages of being vegan.

They are questions laced with guilt.

They imply: 'How could you do this to yourself? Health is a serious matter and you should know exactly what you're doing before taking your long-term health in your own hands.'

They indicate that being vegan requires an extensive understanding of the human metabolism, well above that of 'normal' men and women.

Like I said earlier, a healthy vegan does not need an encyclopaedic knowledge of anything and that includes carbohydrates, fats, proteins, essential minerals, vitamins, calorie conversion rates or the host of human ailments available to everyone.

Again, reach for commonsense as your backstop and seek advice when unsure or have specific health problems.

Even though I have been vegan since the year 2000 I haven't memorised responses to satisfy every determined inquisitor.

Could I anyway?

When stumped I attempt to admit my failing, listen to a criticism or concern and later seek answers that will at least satisfy me about the particular matter in question.

If possible, I then pass some researched information to whoever raised the issue.

There is always more to learn.

So the following nutritional thoughts are based on information gleaned from authoritative sources, including the Queensland and New South Wales vegan societies, other health-based organisations, books and a variety of individuals.

Oh, and some experience.

Previously mentioned author, Michael Klaper, provides a sound catchphrase launching board.

'Humans,' he says 'can derive all of their essential nutrients from a plant-based diet'.

That said, there is a rider he recognises that deserves particular attention, a sort of nutritional bogeyman skulking in the vegan underworld—vitamin B12.

Let's look at it.

和

facing a bogey
(vitamin b12 and nutrition)

Vitamin B12 can be scary.

A lack of it, that is.

It's the only vitamin not considered to be reliably available to humans from eating a varied plant-based diet, with adequate fruit and vegetables and reasonable exercise and exposure to sunlight.

Yes, it's significant, but don't let the bogeyman scare you to death.

Most of us are not eeking along under constant threat of B12 deficiency.

It's a nutrient of potential concern to everyone, though it's not an issue for most people who eat a diversity of foods, keep active and monitor it along with their other regular health checks.

B12 (or cobalamin as it's also called) is often thrown up when the health of vegans is under scrutiny.

But problems associated with a lack of it are not restricted to vegans.

B12 plays a key role in normal brain function, maintenance of our nervous system, formation of red blood cells and thus the prevention of anaemia (tiredness, breathlessness and pale skin).

A deficiency of vitamin B12 can cause brain and nervous system damage, and long-term problems can be irreversible.

Vitamin B12 is also considered essential for pregnant and breastfeeding women

和

and for the healthy growth and development of infants and children.

Because B12 is required by all cells in our bodies deficiency symptoms can be wide ranging or not apparent at all.

Common symptoms can include apathy, memory loss, weight loss, nausea and vomiting, mental confusion, delusions, respiratory problems and allergies.

Vitamin B12 is synthesised by bacteria and is said to be more reliably found in the non-vegan items of meat, dairy products and eggs.

> Whether bacteria are animals or plants is another debate. In fact they're neither in the animalia or plantae kingdoms, because of their basic cell structure they're classified in a micro-organism kingdom called monera.

Be assured, meat eaters too can be deficient in B12, and other essential nutritional elements, depending on their diets.

Surveys, sited by Manuj Chandra in his paper *Vitamin B12 supplementation: natural or unnatural*, indicated as many as 50 per cent of meat eaters and 60 per cent of vegans could be vitamin B12 deficient.

Dr Michael Klaper says that as B12 bacteria are common soil micro-organisms B12 is found in fresh garden vegetables washed and eaten uncooked, some drinking water, fermented foods like tempeh, supplemented plant-based foods and even in our own mouths and intestines.

As a result of today's excessive industrial farming practices, sanitised food processing techniques and antiseptic personal hygiene these are no longer considered 100 per cent guaranteed B12 sources.

Mr Chandra says bacteria in our mouths is being destroyed by anti-bacterial substances in modern toothpaste and dental products and there's virtually no bacteria left in urban water to produce B12 because of it being chlorinated or contaminated by industrial wastes, herbicides and pesticides.

The skin of fruits and vegetables can contain B12 but due to herbicides, pesticides, irradiation, washing, peeling and cooking their skin B12 can be inaccessible to us and washing our hands in soap, gets rid of dirt that contains traces of B12, Mr Chandra says.

Dr Klaper and other authorities agree that while most vegans consume enough B12 to avoid anaemia and nervous system damage they should consider consuming a reliable source from time to time, such as a vitamin B12 supplement or fortified food including soy-based milks and yeast spreads.

There is no global B12 intake standard nor a definitive list of deficiency symptoms.

和

Everyone should make their own inquiries about B12 and get answers that satisfy them.

And that applies to carnivores as much as herbivores.

Here is what I do about B12.

Most importantly, I don't let the bogeyman spook me into thinking that eating dead animals would overcome deficiency risks.

I allow definite steps, rather than dread of danger, carry me forward.

For example, I try to regularly eat plenty of green leafy vegetables (often they don't get a thorough wash) and I have B12 fortified soy milk on my breakfast cereal most mornings.

Conversely, I don't fret if I miss a serving of fortified tucker here and there (for instance, I was lucky enough to travel for a month in undeveloped countries recently and while the food choice was very limited at times I did not have any resultant B12 issues).

I've thrown the anxiety of B12 deficiency in with many things stashed at the back of my mind, like a sock in a bedroom drawer.

The consequences of inadequate B12 are real enough, but I'm not allowing them to creep into a Frankenstein's monster category.

Deficiency is a potential problem resulting from an extended period of questionable eating and living practices, not a case of miss it today and you're sick tomorrow.

Planning eases my mind.

Once a year I have a blood test to check B12 along with a variety of things such as my prostate antigen, 'good' and 'bad' cholesterol, iron, magnesium, calcium and a stack of other pathological indicators.

As a fit youngster I would have thought that excessive but, as a fit not quite so young anymore, I see it as a safeguard rather than fanaticism,

I'm not a zealot.

I'm not.

Usually I only have to skim over the results then continue on normally with life.

Really, the blood test needle feels the same in my arm whether or not the extracted blood is used to check lots of things or just one.

There is an acceptable range for all the indicators I've just mentioned and if the results show up outside their little boxes, or are substantially different from previous tests, I get medical advice from my local doctor.

Ordinarily the whole thing is uneventful routine.

I see the doctor for a blood test referral, go to a pathologist and whinge about feared pain of needles, nurse gives her reassurances,

和

surprisingly I don't die of needle stick trauma, doctor gets the results and says everything is fine and we do it all again next year.

~~

The first B12 blood test I had, several years after becoming vegan, showed my level was at the low end of the range so I began eating a common fortified yeast spread on toast or bread every day and had a follow-up blood test three months later.

The second test showed my B12 reading had gone through the roof.

As there was more than enough floating around my system I backed off the spread and, at the time of writing this, haven't eaten fortified yeast spread for many years.

My B12 peace of mind comes from that annual blood test, maintaining fortified soy milk for breakfast and keeping a general eye on my varied menu to ensure greens are a popular feature.

Many subsequent annual tests have shown my B12 to be consistently where we'd all like it to be, at the high end of the acceptable range.

It's not a worry.

In fact it usually only crosses my mind with the once a year blood test reminder on the calendar. (And I think about that jolly blood test needle.)

Here's another reassurance, from microbiologist author Richard Lacey.

In his book *Hard to Swallow* he says B12 can be stored for months or years in the human liver.

'People who are unable to absorb this vitamin from their diet, and so suffer pernicious anaemia, can be treated by an injection of B12 as infrequently as once a year.

'It might be better, therefore, to look at the intake of B vitamins (and others, for that matter) on a weekly or a monthly basis, rather than daily.

'The great majority of diets will then be found to contain adequate B vitamins, when reviewed over the longer term,' Professor Lacey says.

To sum up B12 I'd say don't be obsessive, eat and drink food it's in and include it in your regular monitoring and chats with your doctor.

Now, let's skip through a few other nutritional factors.

Protein: Almost all foods contain it.

You'll get plenty from a varied diet including tofu, legumes (for example, beans, peas, soy products), grains (wholegrain breads, brown rice, cereals), greens (such as spinach, broccoli), seeds and nuts (including almonds, nut and tahini spreads).

Abundant protein is available from regularly eating these sort of foods on their own and if you combine them your body's protein absorption rate increases.

和

Vitamin D: This hormone, made through our body's exposure to sunlight, allows us to absorb calcium from food in our intestines. The absorption of calcium is essential for bone strength.

Vitamin D deficiency, once rare in Australia, has become more common since the advent of sunscreen.

Our skin needs to be bare, not sunscreen coated, to get a vitamin D boost from sunlight.

A varied diet and three or four hours out in the sun each week should ensure most people's vitamin D level is adequate. If vitamin D is in a processed product, D2 is the vegan version and D3 is not, it comes from sheep wool.

Calcium: This element is used to build and maintain healthy bones and teeth and is needed for blood clotting and good muscle function.

It is available in greens such as kale, parsley, broccoli and beans plus cauliflower, figs, almonds and tahini. Our body's calcium requirements and the maintenance of healthy bones are also assisted by weight-bearing exercise.

Consuming plenty of calcium won't guarantee strong bones.

Weight-bearing exercise most beneficial for our bones includes walking, running, skipping, dancing and other sports and activities.

Our feet impacting on the ground sends vibrations up through our skeleton, stimulating cells that build bone.

Vitamins A, B, C and E. These are essential for growth, the nervous system, skin and blood vessels, sight, digestion, stamina and our reproductive system.

Look to raw or steamed green vegetables such as spinach, beans, sprouts and cabbages, yellow vegetables including pumpkin, carrots, corn and squash and whole grain cereals, wheat and yeast products, capsicums, tomatoes and citrus fruits.

Sprouting beans and grains can increase their vitamin C content by as much as 600 per cent after about four days and vitamin C improves the absorption of iron in our intestines.

Iron: This element is necessary for healthy blood and regulating body processes.

It is found in the likes of whole grain cereals, dark green leafy vegetables, soy flour, seeds, nuts and pulses such as lentils, beans and peas. Parsley also is high in iron.

Zinc: This mineral helps maintain our immune system and healthy skin. Deficiencies are indicated by white spots on our fingernails. Eating leafy green vegetables, wholegrain products, nuts, mushrooms and legumes including beans and peas should keep you out of strife.

和

Fibre: This cellulose, and other undigested matter, is great for the vessels and ducts that conduct fluids around our bodies.

Your veins, arteries and intestines for instance will love you regularly eating unrefined foods such as cereals.

Fats and oils: They provide energy and help with the absorption of fat soluble calcium and vitamins. Nuts, grains, cereals, pulses and oils extracted from these foods contain all the fats you need.

As they can have double the number of calories, compared with protein and carbohydrate foods, a balanced diet means consuming them in moderation rather than in excess.

Omega 3: These polyunsaturated fatty acids are required for the formation of new tissues in our bodies. Ground linseed oil (also known as flaxseed or flaxseed oil) is considered one of the better vegan sources. Other sources include avocadoes, potatoes, pasta, broccoli, peas, soy products and rice.

Wholegrain foods: These reduce the risk of heart attack, strokes, high blood sugar and other health conditions. Wheat, rice and oat brans are high in fibre, which is associated with better bowel health. Wheat germ is a good source of vitamin E plus iron, magnesium, zinc, potassium and B vitamins.

Alkaline/acid balance (known chemically as pH): A good alkaline level will improve your energy levels and mental clarity, helps your body build bone, retain calcium and reduce soft tissue degeneration and joint inflammation. Maintain alkalinity by replacing processed, salty, sugary and overcooked foods with fresh green vegetables such as asparagus, broccoli and parsley and fruits like watermelon, lime and grapefruit. Other good alkaline foods include rice, grapes, apples, green beans, sweet potato, celery, almonds and linseed (flaxseed) oil.

Raw foods: These are full of enzymes and nutrients that boost our immune system and combat cancer, heart disease, diabetes, obesity and other health problems.

~~

At first blush it can be overwhelming and very confusing when we consciously consider in detail what is good to eat and drink and what is best to avoid.

Draw a deep breath and stick with it though.

You should soon see the maze become a map and the world outside veganism more like a labyrinth of bewilderment.

Confusion diminishes as we simplify our approach to life and focus on facts.

For instance, when thirsty, reach for water.

Investigate the cost of installing a rainwater tank.

和

Bottled water may be fashionable but it's as dear as poison (well as dear as petrol or beer anyway), its throw-away containers and polluting distribution network make it an environmental nightmare and in the main in Australia, it's no safer or better for us than the stuff out of our taps.

So, I carry a reusable stainless steel bottle and refill it regularly.

Water: Unadulterated drinking water is the most overlooked health ingredient in society today, I think.

It's an essential for life as every cell in our bodies needs it to absorb nutrients and expel waste.

It can also improve our minds, increase energy, boost our immune system, relieve pain, improve our looks, aid digestion, give us better movement, reduce hunger, overcome constipation, help reduce some cancer risks and save us money.

Every cell in our bodies has a high proportion of water and every day this is diminished through urination, faeces, respiration (breathing) and evaporation through our skin (sweating).

Water carries oxygen to our cells and this enables our muscles to work harder and longer and grow stronger.

Our brain needs oxygen, and the water we drink and foods we eat (such as raw fruits and vegetables which are dense in water), provides the oxygen to enable us to function at optimum levels so we think and concentrate better, are generally more alert and have greater energy.

Water also keeps our electrolyte levels regulated so our nerves best relay messages to and from our brains.

It provides moisture for our joints that need to be lubricated to stay flexible and pain free, drinking plenty also prevents our bodies retaining fluids and this means it's helping burn fat and flush out toxins.

If we're not drinking enough our liver helps our kidneys deal with toxins but when we're drinking enough our kidneys don't need help and so our liver is able to break down stored fat more efficiently.

Will I go on?

Adequate water also moisturises our skin, reducing wrinkles and helping regulate our body temperature and transport all sorts of nutrients to our organs and tissues.

It is absolutely necessary for our digestion of food and has been associated with improved immunity to sickness, headache prevention and reduced risk of cancers and ailments such as heart attack.

What then would be an adequate amount to drink daily?

Some boffin somewhere came up with the magic number of eight glasses.

和

That seems excessive, but if you're a big bloke doing a hard day's physical labour it may not be enough.

Obviously it depends on your size and activity level.

I try to start each day with a good drink and be aware that I need it continually, especially when I'm outside working more than inside being sedentary.

Symptoms of mild dehydration include thirst, pains in muscles and joints, constipation and headaches along with yellow and strong smelling urine.

If beer, wine, aerated fizzy and 'energy' drinks, processed fruit juices, tea or coffee are more to your taste make some inquiries about what else they contain or what they can do to you, and then partake of your drop sparingly.

I see alcoholic drinks as the drug they are and no longer reach for the social crutch.

Alcohol interferes with brain functions that not only allow us to communicate with the outside world but also coordinate the smooth running of our internal organs.

And some studies link it to increased cancer risks.

With no longer any desire to add intoxication of the brain to my limitations, I gave it away entirely in 2000, about the same time as I became a vegan.

You may be shocked to learn what goes into common products such as alcoholic drinks.

Animal bits and pieces, including parts of fish bladders, the white of eggs and fragments of lobster and crab shells can be used in the cleansing process of some beer and wine.

Why?

I wouldn't have a clue.

Such antiquated practice is not a necessity.

Animals don't have to die so beer and wine can be filtered.

To find out what is in various products, such as drinks, talk to long-time vegan beer and wine drinkers, contact a vegan group or even a food or drink manufacturer and ask: 'Is such and such vegan?'

If you don't get a clear answer, don't use the stuff.

Then tell the seller or manufacturer so and invite them to let you know if, or when, it is vegan so you could resume purchasing their product.

Vegan-friendly natural beers and organic wines are readily available.

Some 'energy' drinks, tea and coffee contain caffeine which is a stimulant and diuretic that increases our water loss through urine.

Fizzy 'soft drinks' may not be quite as bad in the cruelty-free stakes as other beverages or animal based foodstuffs but they can be absolutely loaded with sugars which are a stepping stone to tooth decay and the chronic conditions of obesity and diabetes.

和

Sugar in itself isn't so much of a problem.

It's the amount we consume.

As Professor Lacey points out, the human body can quite easily make sugar from other substances, such as starch, which comes in foods such as potatoes and cereals, and they need no extraction or processing.

And please, don't overlook the value of sufficient exercise in maintaining health.

Just 30 minutes, five days a week helps keep your body ticking along properly and combat obesity, diabetes, a variety of cancers, osteoporosis and heart disease.

Health in our affluent society is so closely linked to everyday lifestyle choices, The World Health Organisation's *February 2014 World Health Report* reiterated.

It confirmed that cancer had overtaken heart disease as the biggest killer in Australia, and globally.

About cancers, the organisation's director-general, Margaret Chan, wrote in the report 'Those associated with the world of poverty, including infection-related cancers, are still common, while those associated with the world of plenty are increasingly prevalent, owing to the adoption of industrialised lifestyles with increasing use of tobacco, consumption of alcohol and highly processed foods and a lack of physical activity.'

和

under the skin
(food additives)

Sorry, but in the early stages of being vegan you should read food and drink labels.

Yes it's tedious.

Once you get the hang of what's vegan and what isn't though you can largely put label surfing aside.

Focus on your needs, and its variety, instead of commercialism's ever expanding availability jumble.

Soon you won't have to even glance at non-vegan products in the main.

You'll just occasionally check out new or interesting items and foodstuffs that catch your eye.

To a degree it's right not to fret over all the little things in life as we have bigger things to attend to, though that's different to paying attention to detail and establishing basic good habits.

If you spend some initial time to get little things sorted you'll set a strong foundation from which to approach immense challenges.

Not only are supermarket food labels dull, they too often provide limited enlightenment.

For a concise understanding of what is in processed and packaged items you will need a small ingredient de-coding book that explains food additives.

和

These handy number crunchers aren't hard to find and they are indispensable for interpreting what's actually in that can, bottle or packet you're picked up.

What's under the label could soon be under your skin if you're not careful.

Discovering the junk that goes into some packaged and processed foods and drinks astonished me.

There are about 4000 known substances that can be added to food sold in Australia.

For a confusing array of reasons they all don't have to be disclosed.

'Approved' additives must appear on labels though.

Additives are an assortment of chemical and natural substances used to extend the shelf life of foods, supposedly enhance texture and taste, preserve, sweeten, colour, bleach, thicken and thin down foods and drinks.

They are not all bad.

They are not all good either.

And they are not in all foods.

Thankfully, in response to community concerns about vegan and vegetarian diets, animal cruelty, human obesity and environmental impacts, an increasing contingent of manufacturers are reducing and even eliminating unnecessary additives from products.

But there's a long way to go.

Salt and sugar are the most common additives in processed and packaged foods.

They help preserve food, although too much sugar makes people fat, causes tooth decay and is associated with one of Australia's fastest growing diseases, diabetes, which can lead to heart attack, blindness and stroke.

Too much salt contributes to high blood pressure and is a risk factor for serious heart problems and kidney disorders.

Colourings and flavourings also stand out on manufacturer use lists.

There are three types of colours and flavours, natural, those synthesised to mimic the natural and the third lot are chemical compounds not found in nature.

Flavourings, such as spices, aim to enhance the taste of a meal and other products.

Colouring is added with the aim of making food appear more appetising.

There are hundreds of approved and widely used additives.

Are they all necessary?

Are they all avoidable?

And what do they do to you?

To these questions I'd say no, no and who really knows half the jolly time.

Often people don't even realise there are additives in foodstuffs, let alone potentially harmful ones, until they cause an adverse reaction.

和

Additives are approved by representatives of government authorities with the intention of having an overall positive affect on food quality or appearance.

By the same token, the generalised approval system cannot take infallible account of people's individual diets, allergies or medical problems, including kidney and liver ailments, asthma, hyperactivity or the impact of excessive amounts of particular foodstuffs or particular additives on some infants, children and adults.

Manufacturers can either name a particular additive on their label (such as *bone phosphate)* or list its approved number, for example, 542.

No prizes, in this case, for guessing which description most of them go for.

Who among the general population would bother looking up what a number stood for?

But for those wondering, bone phosphate is calcium extracted from animal bones.

It is an 'anti-caking agent' that is meant to reduce food particles sticking together and help salt disperse in products.

It can be used as a mineral supplement, a 'filler' in tablets and in dried and powdered cow's milk.

Additives in Australian food and drinks have numbers in line with a more extensive European list.

Additives from 100 to 181 are colours, 200 to 297 are preservatives and food acids, 300 to 381 are anti-oxidants, mineral salts and food acids, 400 to 579 are emulsifiers, firming agents, stabilisers, anti-caking agents, humecants, mineral salts and vegetable gums, 620 to 637 are flavour enhancers, 900 to 1202 are sweeteners, bleaches, propellants plus glazing and anti-foaming agents, 1400 to 1450 are thickeners, 1505 to 1520 are solvents and sequestrants.

It's mind boggling.

Honestly, who in their right mind would have a clue what a humecant or sequestrant was?

So, lets unscramble it a bit by looking at a few numbers that caught my attention when thumbing through two books—*Food Additives* by Sue Treffers and *The New Additive Code Breaker* by Maurice Hanssen, Jill Marsden and Betty Norris.

102 is **tartrazine**, a synthetic azo dye used for yellow and other colours. It is very commonly used in 'soft' drinks, confectionary, packet dessert toppings and canned peas.

This synthetic substance is considered the most reactive azo dye.

It is known to cause migraine headaches, skin rashes, allergic reactions in hyperactive children and cross react with salts in the pain relief drug asprin.

和

120 is **cochineal**, a water soluble red colouring used for liquids, including alcoholic drinks.

This colour is made by crushing up the bodies of pregnant scale insects which eat cacti in central and South America.

Cochineal is possibly toxic to unborn babies and has been linked to hypersensitivity, especially in children.

322 is **lecithin**, which is used to allow fats, oils and water to mix better in items like chocolate, confectionery, margarine and mayonnaise.

While most commercial lecithin is derived from soya beans it can also obtained from animal products such as chicken egg yolks.

441 is **gelatine**, which has now been defined as a food, rather than an additive, and the name should be listed as a food ingredient.

It is obtained by boiling down animal parts that contain collagen, such as the skin of pigs and cattle, hoofs, bone and ligaments.

Gelatine is used as a food stabiliser, thickener and emulsifier forming the basis of jellies and glues.

Its side effects can include allergic reactions, lowering blood pressure and decreasing resistance to infection.

469 is **casein sodium.** This is a stabiliser, emulsifier, binder and whitener used in beverages, cheeses, dessert mixes and thickened cream.

It is the major protein in cow's milk.

621 is **monosodium glutamate**, *(commonly referred to as MSG)*. This salt is used in cooking to enhance flavours.

MSG comes from glutamic acid in plant and animal tissues, including all sorts of meat and cow's milk.

Most of today's MSG is said to be manufactured from plants.

MSG is typically found in some 'fast' foods, packet soups, sauces and flavoured noodles.

Sue Treffer's work, *Food Additives*, says MSG is not suitable for infants or small children, could be dangerous for asthmatics and asprin sensitive people and possibly cause allergic reactions, including heart palpitations, nausea and headaches.

901 is **beeswax**. This wax is secreted by these insects with the intention of constructing honeycomb.

We humans use it in our food as a polish and glazing agent for fruit and to flavour confectionary, beverages, commercial baked products and ice cream.

Resin in the wax has been known to cause occasional hypersensitivity reactions.

904 is **shellac**. This is used as a glazing agent for fruit and confectionary.

This is a reddish substance produced by mealy bug-type insects from Southern Asia.

和

One of the four commercial grades of shellac includes some of the potentially poisonous compound arsenic.

Shellac may cause skin irritation.

920 is **L-cysteine**. It is a flavourer, especially for chicken flavour, and a flour treatment agent that can be used in breadmaking.

It is made from animal hair and chicken feathers, and in China can include human hair.

Some additives react with other additives and some are created from chemicals you're never likely to have heard of and things you'd never suspect, such as petroleum, or in the case of an extremely common sugar substitute—it's an artificial chemical derived from coal tar.

In addition to food and drink, animals are also used as ingredients in, or pre-human testers for, daily household items including toiletries and cosmetics.

Ah yes, animal testing.

It's based on the questionable belief that experiments on animals can be directly related to humans.

Hundreds of thousands of consumer items, from processed food to industrial chemicals, are understood to have required animal tests before human use.

Rabbits, rats, mice and dogs are the usual ones to suffer so we can be assured that a fizzy drink, hair product, food preservative, or some other modern day 'essential' is safe for our consumption.

'We wouldn't be able to develop such and such for the benefit of mankind without animal testing,' is the industry's catchcry.

It's a pathetic excuse.

Again, read the labels and if they aren't clear or you suspect ingredient euphemisms are glossing over animal testing, ask questions and don't use the product until your queries are satisfied.

和

tree of life
(from neanderthal to genetic engineering)

Genetically engineered (GE) food is a topic that deserves vegan attention, and to assist our squinting into a microscope at it I'd like to glance back in time.

Human cave dwellers in a distant primitive epoch known as the Palaeolithic era are credited with developing simple chipped-stone implements to improve their existence.

They opened their account by devising tools of flint, like a wood-chopping axe for instance.

With subsequent axes more fragments were knocked off the flint edges to make newer models more efficient.

The spark of progress was ignited.

Improvements gradually spread to a variety of endeavours, each building on the previous.

Microbiologist author Richard Lacey says in his book *Hard to Swallow*, that our ancestor Homo sapiens began growing crops and controlling animals and birds for food about 6000 years ago.

Eventually metal replaced stone and more modified utensils and equipment transformed whole living environments as the breadth of change and life's pace quickened.

Difficulties were pursued by solutions.

和

Humanity embraced 'civilization', which was refined by subsequent generations.

Professor Lacey says the desirability and yield of plants was increased along with animals that were 'improved' by human selection and hydridisation.

Micro-organisms such as bacteria and yeasts were exploited.

Brewing and cheese making are part of our ancient history, along with the use of early food preservatives—drying and the use of salt and sugar, he says.

Farm folk around Egypt's river Nile were drafted to erect pyramids.

Empires rose and fell: Persia, the Romans, Aztecs and Vikings.

There were peasants, explorers, heroes and warmongers.

History was painted by the meagre, as well as the magnificent.

Revolution swept into France, Russia and then America.

By 1914 the world had reached its 'war to end all wars' and then in 1945 the glow of nuclear radiation settled over more than the decimated Japanese cities of Hiroshima and Nagasaki.

Progress had reached a pivotal point.

The human race now held exceptional, almost unbelievable power.

We had worked out a way to harness extraordinary energy from atoms, one of the smallest elements of life.

The realisation was dazzling, yet the holocaust outcome of atomic bombs which ended World War II shocked even the nation which dropped them.

There was solemn reflection.

Though in a seemingly short period, among all the swirling emotions, came mankind's desire to march on.

And the latest 'new world order' embraced the unrelenting confidence that coexists with progress.

For progress is oiled by an underlying good intent and rhetoric about addressing past wrongs and improving the lot of all.

The bombs had to be dropped, said the bombers.

Our Neanderthal forefathers had developed into pinstriped politicians and a white-coated class of technologists in laboratories.

Along with rebuilding World War II's global devastation, 'progress' resumed its merry course.

Technobabblers scrambled back onto their pedestals.

On a material level, plastics gradually replaced many metals.

Cybernetics and a myriad of esoteric endeavours gained scientific prominence.

和

They were borne on more words of good intent—to advance humanity.

One strand of this was the 'improving and securing' of world food supplies.

To defer to Professor Lacey again, he says: 'But improvements in crops and food animals were slow in bygone eras, and the technological changes in our food production over the last 70—80 years have been much more dramatic than in the previous 30 million'.

The practice of artificial insemination has revolutionised animal husbandry, both in breeding and rearing.

Artificial fertilisers, chemicals to fight pests and genetic engineering have enabled us to produce substantially more food than previously from the same space.

Genetic engineering, Professor Lacey says, is a technique dating back to the 1970s and is very much an American invention.

Although it is these days still hawked with warm and fuzzy promotional gloves, it concerns me greatly, and not through ignorance or even a fear of mutation.

Genetic engineering is the technical alteration of basic cells that form life.

Scientists take infinitesimally tiny pieces (genes) from one life form and insert them into another.

Minute parts of bacteria, for instance, can be inserted into a seed to change characteristics of its offspring.

It is more than merely growing plants to better tolerate droughts or make food items look prettier and last longer on supermarket shelves.

Genetic engineering leaves for dead natural selection and old fashioned farming processes of selective breeding.

Natural selection occurs when individuals of a particular species breed.

A species is a line of plants or animals related by common ancestry.

Selective breeding involves farmers choosing plants with desirable characteristics to produce the next generation, for example, crossing a mildew-resistant grape with a high-yielding grape with the intention of having progeny with some of both desirable characteristics.

Genetic engineering crosses not only the species barrier but tampers with the tree of life.

For example, genes from fishes that live in very cold seas could to be inserted into strawberries, enabling new fruit to be more frost-tolerant.

An experiment along these lines is explained in a 2010 'fact sheet' published by Better Health Channel in consultation with, and approval from, Australia's Deakin University.

和

The document says the GE fish and strawberry mating feat has, as yet, not been perfected for currently available commercial food crops.

The experiment continues.

The tree of life, as defined by centuries of scientific research, is the categorising of the tremendous diversity of species on earth into related kingdoms.

Basically the tree of life outlines human biological reasoning that sets apart animals and plants, life forms that can reproduce themselves independently and other tiny organisms without a distinct nucleus.

Genetic engineering slices these boundaries into confetti.

It is also a technology that allows multinational companies to own and control certain forms of life.

At present a handful of huge chemical companies dominate the GE industry.

And with, I believe, limited long-term health and environmental testing, GE products have been introduced into our global food chain.

It may already be an unstoppable phenomenon.

People who support genetic engineering contend that the world's growing human population needs inexpensive, safe and nutritious foods.

Who could argue against that?

Well, before I have a go, let's run through some of what else supporters say.

GE plants could better withstand weather extremes, taste nicer, last longer and be instilled with things such as healthy antioxidants and medicinal vaccines.

GE crops resistant to disease and pests could reduce the amount of chemicals sprayed on farm produce and correspondingly lower food and environmental contamination.

All commendable objectives.

And humanity has always had a need for nutritious, inexpensive, safe food and, I'm convinced, always had an ability to meet it.

Commonsense dictates that it's inconceivable for genetic engineers to give an enduring and serviceable guarantee that what they are creating will have no adverse catastrophic consequences.

Our greed and other self-centred obstacles, rather than a lack of natural means or technological know-how, are really why the rich are dying of obesity while millions of poor people the world over starve to death every year.

It would be admirable if GE promises materialised, although I fail to see how having fewer and fewer people (the corporate chiefs) with more and more power could lead to all people in need of nutritious, inexpensive, safe food actually receiving it.

和

Such an altruistic regard strikes me as the jingoistic patter of commercialism.

Will the world food market really benefit?

I think it's more likely that corporate legal constraints will further reduce seed saving for traditional farmers and home gardeners and cut plant access for the poor in underprivileged countries.

GE plants that include animal genes cause an ethical dilemma for vegans and others concerned about animal welfare and adulterated foods.

Fruit and vegetables, born of the genetic material of pigs and cows, may be offensive to people of certain cultural and traditional religious beliefs.

Concerns also spread to GE foods extending human allergic reactions and reducing the effectiveness of medical antibiotics, thus increasing human infectious disease risks.

Then there is the possible hazard of cross-breeding between GE crops and surrounding vegetation, contaminated weeds and insects becoming herbicide and pesticide resistant and the possibility of GE material having an adverse impact on GE-free crops as well as native flora and fauna biodiversity.

GE substances may already be affecting indispensible crop pollinating insects such as bees.

The environmental organisation Greenpeace has been campaigning for GE-free foods, stringent safety testing and comprehensive labelling in Australia since 2003 with what the group calls its *Truefood Guide.*

Greenpeace spokeswoman Laura Kelly told me that shoppers expressing their view and buying GE-free foods have had a major impact on the penetration of GE foods in Australia.

More than half the country's top food companies have established GE-free food policies since the first *Truefood Guide* was released, she said.

At the time of writing this, fresh vegetables and fruit in Australia, along with all certified organic food and wines in the country were GE-free.

On the other hand, all cottonseed oils and all imported vegetable oils may contain GE material.

While current Australian food regulations require pre-market assessments so that only 'safe' GE products (as nutritious as conventional counterparts) are sold in the country, there is plenty of grey packaging around the technology.

The Better Health fact sheet, for instance, says the safety of GE foods remains in dispute 'as it is impossible to predict all of the potential effects on human health and the environment.

'Some public health experts advocate caution.

'They believe that we are at a scientific starting line,' says the fact sheet.

和

Australian GE food labelling laws only apply to some modified ingredients, additives and processing substances.

GE warning labels are not required for point of sale food such as takeaway shops, bakeries and restaurants.

Labels are not required for highly refined foods (such as cooking oil from modified corn, sugars or starches) and food flavours consisting less than .1 per cent of a product or food and its ingredients that are 'unintentionally' present in less than one per cent of food.

A stack of GE soy and corn from America is imported into Australia as processed ingredients in stockfeed, so if you avoid meat eating you'll avoid at least some potential flow-on of GE material.

The main sources of GE foods in Australia at present are chocolates, bread, biscuits, potato chips, margarine and mayonnaise that include soya imported from America which has been genetically engineered to survive certain chemical herbicides.

Other GE food sources in our country include cottonseed oil (made from pesticide-resistant cotton) used for frying, commercial salad dressings and mayonnaise, plus GE corn that has arrived in imported processed items such as breakfast cereal, corn chips, bread and gravy mixes.

And on the agricultural front, battlelines were drawn in January 2011 when West Australian organic farmer Steve Marsh confirmed he would take legal action after losing organic certification in 2010 because of GE contamination from a nearby farm.

His wheat and oat crops were downgraded to lower-priced conventional status because 70 per cent of his 478 hectare property was contaminated by 'Roundup Ready Canola', a herbicide resistant variety of rapeseed owned by the giant American-based GE and chemical company Monsanto.

This was the first time an Australian organic farmer had lost certification as a result of GE contamination.

West Australian Agricultural Minister Terry Redman told Mr Marsh that zero tolerance of GE material in organic crops was 'unrealistic' and Monsanto officials announced the company would bankroll the GE farming community's legal defence.

In April 2012, Steve Marsh lodged a West Australian Supreme Court writ, suing for losses and a permanent injunction to protect his farm from more contamination.

In 2014 he lost the case, had an $800,000 legal bill and appealed the verdict. As I write, it was unresolved.

The matter will greatly influence whether Australian farmers can grow GE-free crops.

和

on the hoof
(livestock links)

Conflict is an absolute requirement of our being.

Only the form, depth and frequency of discord vary.

How we deal with this unavoidable trait is what sets humans apart from each other.

Some of us struggle every day, some glide through it, some are presented with more than a fair share of troubles while a few others revel in it.

Once I watched a professional Irish boxer who blessed himself with a sign of the cross as he faced his opponent.

He prayed for god's speed, and that's fine because that was not all he relied upon when entering the ring.

He sure knew how to throw a punch.

His particular contest was intentional, and he was ready.

But fair dinkum, fighting, regardless of whether it's a physical or mental stoush is not where most of us prefer to be, especially on a regular basis.

It may be okay in some circles as an entertainment spectacle, but I think it's a pity that conflict wasn't constricted by more than pugilist ropes.

Although I'm no fisticuffs fan I know that a degree of tension in our lives, and sometimes serious disputes, can eventually produce good.

Confronting a difficulty makes us focus on what's important, examine where we're headed, and even if we're not prepared for sudden conflict, hopefully

和

we have time to reflect on the consequences and then step accordingly.

It strengthens our purpose.

One of my greatest causes for strife in life has been embedded in a regard for what we as humans are doing to our environment.

That upset has increasingly come to rotate around the livestock industry.

To put it mildly, I'm frustrated by the lack of concern about animal slaughter for meat and other products, and associated ecological desecration.

Whether we're vegan ninjas or not, I wonder, how even the most cunning and crafty among us could assail mankind's destructive tendencies?

Life is complicated.

Laying the industry to rest today would do much to bring me peace of mind.

Regretfully though I'm not the sole arbiter.

And no matter who the arbiter may be, decisively coming to terms with livestock's impacts will not be a painless process.

In fact an abrupt shutdown could cause more problems than it solved.

Livestock's links to mankind's life is also complicated.

Impacts cannot be reasonably assessed in isolation.

A lot rides on the backs of animals.

While millions of people throughout the world have largely cut themselves free of meat and more could do the same right now if they wished, substantial historic circumstances prevent the industry's immediate wholesale dismantling.

Swathes of humanity are hobbled to it as surely as poor beasts in factory farms.

And while health and environmental authorities have for years advised people to reduce meat eating, or even become vegan or vegetarian, it's not possible to unequivocally calculate the net global effect of a meat-free world, compared to a meat-based existence.

No doubt, I believe, there is an overall benefit, it's just not a simple black and white equation.

Release from the mire relies on recognition of encompassing factors and then constructively wading through them.

A just transition from this violent and wasteful food source seems only possible if the general populace has an understanding that becomes a will to develop alternatives to deal with reality.

Hopefully, supporters of the livestock industry eventually accept its negativities, just as those opposed to it have to recognise its benefits and tangible long-term connections with humanity.

Much of the economy in developed countries depends on the meat trade so there are powerful vested interest sectors that don't want it to do anything but increase.

和

And just as the effect of rising sea levels will impact heavily on people in the world's poorest countries, stopping the meat trade will also hit them hardest.

Livestock is a significant contributor in developing countries, providing food and income for one billion of the world's poorest people.

In Asia and Africa, in particular, livestock is virtually the only source of livelihood for some and a lack of other practical choices at this stage causes major headaches for social and political decision makers.

More than 12 per cent of the global population (870 million people) is undernourished, the international programs director for the aid organisation Caritas Australia, Jamie Davies, said in September 2013.

Almost all these people live in developing countries.

And, on average, they spend 70 per cent of their daily income on food.

The United Nations reports that as many as eight million children die every year from malnutrition and preventable diseases such as diarrhoea, malaria and measles.

How offensive is this when humans produce enough food for everyone and we in wealthy countries are killing ourselves through overeating.

Ms Davies said her organisation focused on 'sustainable livelihoods and food security for the poorest of the poor.'

That focus, she said, not only covered help with access to nutritious food, clean water, appropriate seeds, tools, sustainable agriculture training, better irrigation systems and markets, it had to include animal husbandry and empowering people to catch their own fish for food.

The marginalised deserve leeway, I say, while blowtorch scrutiny should be turned on us, the rich, what we're doing with our disproportionate cut and our push to profitably expand into developing countries.

The overall increasing demand for meat and animal products throughout the world is being driven by our growing human population, spreading urbanisation plus greater worldwide financial incomes.

Global meat production is predicted to double from about 230 million tonnes in 2001 to about 465 million tonnes by 2050 when our earth will have to support about nine billion people.

Most demand growth for meat is predicted to come from India, China and Brazil while pigs and poultry are tipped to be the prime cuts ahead of cattle, sheep and goats.

At present, Australia is the second-biggest beef export country in the world, behind Brazil, with cattle having an annual farm gate value of at least $7.5billion.

和

About 65 per cent of the Australian countryside is managed by farmers, with around 95 per cent of this agricultural land used for meat production.

Although there are vegetarian alternatives, meat has an undeniable nutritional value for the bulk of our population, particularly as a source of protein and minerals such as iron and zinc.

Also, right-minded livestock farmers can provide a positive environmental impact through land management that restores flora and fauna biodiversity, captures climate changing carbon and reduces sedimentation of waterways.

Acknowledge this I can, but it rattles like an admission of despair.

Surely farmers could still do good for the environment without farming animals, but how would they make a living?

And how would farms operate?

For instance, even if small-scale, organic vegetable farms that mimicked nature proliferated to supply local demands, where would their soil fertilisers come from if animal manure was not available?

I don't have the answers, but I do know there are answers that do not require mankind's current level of exploitation and destruction.

The other side of debate on the livestock chain is that it is one of humanity's major climate change accelerators through deforestation, transport and energy use, land degradation, animal waste fermentation and its filth from processing.

Farting and belching alone from Australia's livestock is understood to account for about 10 per cent of the country's total greenhouse gas pollution.

Livestock worldwide account for about 10 per cent of humanity's total water use and because of the industry's sheer size it's probably the world's worst commercial sector water polluter through erosion and chemical and manure run-off.

By comparison, production of food for a vegetarian diet requires only half the water used to provide an average omnivore diet that includes meat and dairy products.

But even if everyone in the entire world stopped eating meat this very instant, all the animals aren't going to instantaneously disappear.

They'd still require feed and water and continue farting and belching til the day they died.

Change to more sane global eating habits must be gradual.

Nutritionally, a balanced plant-based vegan diet is better than a typical meat-based diet, but thanks to the meat industry's political, social and advertising clout most Australians don't know it.

和

The livestock industry's utter proportion makes it a permanent and worsening threat to freshwater supplies, land and aquatic ecosystems plus all their native dependants.

By occupying more than 60 per cent of Australia's total land mass, and virtually one in every three hectares throughout the entire world, livestock properties contain massive slices of crucial indigenous ecology and biodiversity.

With so many people relying on livestock for financial incomes and as a food source, political decision makers traditionally bias their judgements towards 'economic necessity' well ahead of environmental, health and social considerations.

And topping all this is the media hurdle.

Meat is a snugly entrenched customer in advertising circles, turning over more than $13billion a year in Australia and about $500billion throughout the world.

If the meat industry's advertising tally was compared to international economies it would rank just outside the biggest 20, says Jon Casimir in his book, *The Gruen Transfer.*

This is what gives livestock its underlying clout.

Direct meat advertising is a fraction of the total media bling, but indirect broadcasting of meat's message is impossible to extract from the ever expanding matrix.

A macho meat mentality is not just there in hamburger and beer advertisements.

It's often associated with all sorts of foods and a multitude of other products from weight loss and health programs to assorted glamour 'needs' and everyday items from a local playgroup's sausage sizzle right up to international sport event cuisine.

With dexterous images of erotic desire, 'cool', freedom and fashion, advertising shapes the consumer mindset.

And as Australians eat around $9billion worth of meat a year, meat is clearly a mindset staple, Jon Casimir's book attests.

Meat advertisements wreak of sex appeal and vitality, and backed by celebrity endorsement, override the fact that eating animals is not so good for us, or mother earth, as all this media guff makes out.

A 'must eat it' attitude is repeatedly regurgitated.

And the ads work.

For instance, the chiefs of the multinational hamburger corporation McDonalds wouldn't screen more than 130 different Australian television ads annually if they didn't help the company sell one in every 72 commercial meals consumed in the country.

Reality like that can intimidate a bloke like me behind his little vegan ninja mask.

和

The saturation of people's thoughts by a repeated message contributes immensely to why the 'must eat it' view is such a pervasive mainstream notion.

And as an opponent I quake.

I take a breath.

Then, as others do, I push on.

There must be a way to get round this propaganda trickery, I think.

It's encouraging to spot lateral action that confronts the status quo, even if it's small in comparison with the challenge.

Here are a couple of examples.

The conservation group, World Wildlife Fund (WWF), has instigated an innovative program to inject some practical eco-friendly thought and action into the boardrooms of 100 key borderless food producing, retailing and commodity trading enterprises.

They include McDonalds, drink manufacturer Coca-Cola and the mega-marketing group Cargill, and a few of the main target commodities include beef, sugar, palm oil, coffee, cotton and soybeans.

The program highlights how food is produced, as well as how much is needed for our rocketing global population, while apparently still aiming to satisfy escalating environmental, animal welfare, government and changing consumer demands.

WWF spokesman Rob Cairns said the plan sought to reduce the environmental footprint of food by working toward lowering production ecosystem impacts.

Beef tops the hit list, with 'sustainable production' being the program's initial meeting topic in Denver, Colorado, in November 2010.

In April 2011 WWF personnel took part in a sustainable food summit in Melbourne to emphasise environmental and food security issues for inclusion in a national food plan being developed by the Australian Government.

I know many environmental warriors would view 'sustainable production' as unachievable fiction.

Animals are not inanimate objects from which meat is harvested.

A saving grace for such engagement is that potentially warring parties are dealing with their hostilities in a new way.

No doubt it's a long row to hoe before the process bears substantial fruit.

Hopefully though it will bear fruit.

A variety of activists will maintain action on different fronts for sure, regardless of the boardroom banter.

But at least the corporate heads opened discussions with WWF representatives by saying they wanted to be a sizeable part of a solution.

和

At the time of this writing, I give them their due. The process continues.

Food waste is another chunk of the environmental big picture that is also starting to attract serious lateral attention.

David Baker from the political research group, The Australia Institute, presented a paper at an environmental educators conference in Canberra at the end of 2010 calling on government representatives to engage householders and food retailers to help design successful public policy on the issue.

He said Australian households throw away more than $5.2billion worth of food a year yet on an individual level more than half of us think we leave so little uneaten that it's not worth reusing in leftover meals.

Conservatively, every man, woman and child in Australian wastes about $240 of food a year which equates to $1.1billion worth of fruit and vegetables, $1billion from takeaway shops and restaurants, $870million in fresh meat and fish plus $510million in dairy products, Mr Baker said.

From this arises a double-barrelled pollution impact, firstly from emissions involved in the growing, processing and transporting food and secondly when discarded food rots to create the greenhouse accelerant, methane in local government garbage dumps.

Almost half Australia's dump waste is organic material, most of which is household rubbish.

An assessment of garbage dumps found meat products have the largest 'embodied pollution' of any food category—that's all the transport, processing and refrigeration pollution involved in getting meat onto people's plates.

And on a dollar basis, meat's greenhouse gas pollution is nearly 12 times worse than fruit and vegetables.

That means wasted meat products have a far greater environmental impact than any other food, even though we throw away less of it than fruit and vegetables, Mr Baker says.

Australia's total climate changing pollution from household food waste a year is equivalent to the annual emissions from 4.2million cars, or one third of all the passenger vehicles on the nation's roads.

And, it's no surprise, wealthier Australians are more wasteful than lower income earners.

Mr Baker said the connection between economic prosperity and waste (despite a notable individual care factor) was emphasised in a survey of 1600 Australians who were asked what would help them reduce food waste.

和

Eighty five per cent said saving money would be the primary motivator rather than care for the environment. Animal welfare concerns were a distant third motivator.

Doing something substantial to reverse the food waste issue swung not on a lack of worry about waste but on how to translate this concern into behavioural change, Mr Baker said.

Food's ecological footprint will remain a major, and largely ignored, problem until government leaders engage households and food retailers in examining shopping practices and bulk food 'discounts', he said.

Mr Baker said some form of financial incentive should be linked to waste disposal and the community be shown how to save money through small behavioural changes.

I agree, this would be a counterweight to industry advertising and it supports the view that big steps spring from basic observations and what happens each day in ordinary households.

和

baumgarten
(bound to the earth)

There's a tree that snores outside my kitchen window.

Just after daybreak some mornings you can hear its rasping nasal breaths drifting along the edge of our home garden.

In and out, regular and contented.

At first I couldn't work it out.

Then I realised the sound was coming from a fork in the tree, about six metres above the ground.

A young tawny frogmouth owl was there, snuggled up against the trunk fast asleep.

Her plumage was great camouflage and with her head cocked at a peculiar angle she looked like a broken branch, but she didn't have her stealth respiration techniques working smoothly.

Her snuffled gasps seemed magnified as first light inched its way between dawn's speechless shadows.

Yes, I know the silky oak was not really snoring, it was the tawny frogmouth, and tawnies are not strictly owls (they're more closely related to birds of the nocturnal nightjar family), but that's not the point I'm trying to touch.

To me the silky oak will remain a snoring tree because it and this particular bird are so attached.

和

While being physically independent, in many ways they are dependent on each other.

They have a meaningful relationship that demonstrates harmony.

They also illustrate one of humanity's perpetual quests.

We grapple with a need to define ourselves as individuals, to fly free of constraints, yet at the same time wanting a significant bond with life around us—somewhere to snuggle.

It's a pity the snoring tree and tawny frogmouth's natural connection wasn't more widely obvious.

An interconnected web binds all things on earth.

To the casual observer the tree appears to prosper regardless of whether any feathered companions are nestled in its branches.

Such a view though overlooks the value of birds which control insects that feed on plants, help pollinate trees and scatter their seeds so they continue to spread.

And birds rely on trees as food hunting habitats, shady resting spots and safe nesting areas.

There's shared purpose.

Oddly though, our search for meaning in life can carry us astray of shared purpose.

Too often we consider ourselves to be unique individuals and members of a species apart from others.

Human intention is not limited to any specific object nor time so, bolstered by feelings of superiority, we often exact a greater share of what's available around us than our animal and environmental partners.

It's repeated folly we must address.

Additionally, we also too often lack mindful focus.

Put simply, our individual paths lead to where we are at this very moment.

We can only be who we are right now, whatever has preceded.

We may gaze from memories past through a prism of plans and expectations, but today really is the depth of our being.

Each of us abides in the here and now, but our thoughts and actions are too often elsewhere.

Rocking from what has gone before and what's yet to come we fail to fully touch the present and convert that endless pendulum momentum into immediate use.

That's not necessarily perpetually propelling ourselves into action that I'm talking about.

I mean, when we notice our thoughts swinging from one thing to another and another and another, try to be aware that our mind is futilely jumping from one cloud to the next.

Dynamic action may be required on a particular matter, but a myriad of other reactions, right

和

across the spectrum to silent reflection, may be appropriate in our current time.

The crucial ingredient of being present is awareness.

What flows from it is secondary.

The 'balance' we seek in life is nothing more than awareness, being conscious of what we're doing and what we'd like to do.

It reveals the secondary—our ability to choose where next to step.

Trees, whether they snore or not, bring me back to the here and now.

They are grounding, bind me to the earth, and other creatures, and project a sense of constancy.

Perhaps it's their calmness of strength that attracts.

Somehow they remind me that while I'm part of a species whose gross consumer obsessions attack our earth's nervous system, I'm also able to slip out of this relentless onslaught and personally do something to help restore what's being destroyed by our species fateful impact.

As slight and simplistic as it may seem, being roused by trees, and planting them where and when I can, is one way I'm able to stay in the present and realistically weigh the perspective of past and future.

Given a chance, trees can watch over more than one generation, human and otherwise.

And they can save lives.

The Australian heat kills more than 1000 people aged over 65 every year, and climate change is predicted to push this number higher.

An Australian Climate Council report in early 2014 said heatwaves were becoming hotter, longer and more frequent.

It came out shortly after a heatwave in Victoria that resulted in more than 200 deaths being reported to the state coroner.

These deaths were more than twice the state's usual number of deaths for the same period.

Trees, particularly in urban areas, could reduce this impact as they reduce heat, not only through shade, but by taking moisture from the soil and transpiring it through their leaves to humidify and cool surrounding air.

Trees add to my reason for being.

I can't help smiling as I see saplings gain strength from each sunrise and knowing that helping our habitat helps all life.

Tree gardening, as sporadic as mine has been during parts of my life, has nonetheless provided me with a thread of sanity, and an aspect of that illusive 'meaning'.

It has triggered brief, yet lingering, times when I'm acutely awake to my place in nature, when I know that while I'm as small as I think, I'm as big as I feel.

和

And I feel the positive efforts of every individual do make a difference.

At these moments I'm happy.

Or more correctly, it's then I realise the happiness that so often flows for me from so many things.

It has been said, there is no way to happiness, happiness is the way.

To me, this means happiness is an underlying contentment that's highlighted by moments of pleasure.

It's gratitude for the ups and downs that compose life.

Allow me a slight sidetrack.

My wife Julie and I were born within minutes of each other on the same day in the same small Australian country hospital—The Fairholme, in Singleton.

Years later we met, eventually married, had a family of five children and about 20 years on were set to host at our home a youth exchange teenager from Germany.

I thought it would be a nice gesture to plant a few trees on our property to mark the occasion when he arrived.

He landed on our birthday.

He'd come from a part of Germany over which my father Frank's Australian Air Force bomber operated during World War II.

He was born at almost the same time as our son, on the same day, on the other side of the world.

And our youth exchange son's surname was Baumgarten, which translates in English as 'tree garden'.

So, as a family, we planted a handful of trees in a back paddock at Elderslie.

Strangely, it was like meeting for the first time someone we had known forever.

Our connection with nature, with each other and with life surrounding us was so tangible, yet, in the same breath so fleeting.

There's no other way to describe it, we were there and nothing 'outside' seemed to matter even though we knew this feeling was an immediate joy.

It established a physical place we could return to, but more so, it provided a pocketed moment we could draw out time and again in the future.

Happiness was obvious, as was our desire to continue planting.

As a result, our little baumgarten has spread through the years and now I'm held by its forest spell.

I'd love to see baumgartens, patches of greenery that embody the connective tissue of which we're all part, sprouting all over the world.

Gardening in itself is food for the soul.

It doesn't matter whether it is a few trees down the backyard, a humble vegetable plot, lush parkland

和

estate, a flowerbox on an urban windowsill or a spot of guerrilla gardening (irregular, surprise and unofficial planting raids in public and private places, no matter who owns them).

It's all worthwhile and uplifting.

Others may find meaning elsewhere, but planting even one tree does it for me.

Life is without predestined purpose, unalterable purpose that is, outside the extremely basic, such as breathing, eating and drinking, moving, resting, ageing and dying.

We must consciously create meaning or be blown like ghosts to our graves.

Through life, we will be blown anyway, that is unalterable, though the extent is not.

So, let's gather a few garments of intent around us as we dance to the chaos of creation, I say.

We are neither completely locked in to our circumstances nor have the control many people imply by their know-all attitude.

We do have an ability to determine some things of importance to us and there lies hope, even if it appears to be but a tiny increment.

Now, where was I?

Ah yes—the way.

Happiness is the way.

That can be a difficult notion to understand but it makes more sense when viewed as part of our human condition of craving—to become 'someone', do something noteworthy, achieve, acquire and succeed.

Our self-frustrating effort is a wearisome repeat performance.

To a degree, everyone knows our cravings are only momentarily filled by the objects of our wants.

An awakening occurs when we confront ourselves.

Instead of asking 'what will satisfy me now?' try asking 'why am I not satisfied?'

By 'what', I'm thinking of things such as comfort food, a flash pair of joggers, a ski trip to the snow or a new car.

And by 'why' I'm referring to what's prompted a particular want.

Why do I want such and such, what's behind it?

Is it as shallow as an advertising jingle or a deeper malaise such as feeling unloved, facing financial failure or another aspect of the human condition we're trying to avert our attention from?

It's not easy, especially at the start of questioning our 'needs', because often it's not obvious why exactly we're so discontented.

What is beneath this frustration?

Even if an answer isn't evident, simply putting an inquiring halt to an unsatisfactory cycle loosens its grip on our habits.

和

Whether or not we continue striving in a particular way should become more transparent.

We may then understand that one of the main differences between someone who is smart and someone who is not can often be nothing more than one realises it.

Awareness.

Life turns on it.

Savour now rather than be unhappy with what has been or may be.

And if awareness is what we seek, the concept of being vegan is one of many aspects of life that can both become clearer and help in making clearer other parts of our existence.

Vegans don't deal in miracles.

They deal in the day to day.

Sure, the extraordinary can be found in life's magic moments, though it's more lastingly found for the bulk of us through being stirred by the ordinary.

We must continually return to awareness of the present, the meaning and hope in what is before us right now.

Hope does more than combat fear.

It helps build self-respect, which is at the root of compassion.

Hope can get the most poorly of us out of bed each morning and teach us that peace of mind is not some glittering object, it's how we deal with now.

And now is more often than not ordinary.

A life of heroic deeds or a Shaolin monk's contemplative detachment, for example, are far removed from the way my world usually unfolds.

Sometimes it cascades confusingly as I'm consumed by frustrations, anger, time wasting, any number of common daily distractions or reality's unfairness.

That's when the basics of humble, compassionate thought make a difference, when I have something to draw upon and realise that practical steps can cure many ills.

And sometimes my inadequacies just scream in my face.

All tensions are not irreconcilable though.

Try not to be seduced by a hollow pursuit of personal perfection, or any materialistic mecca, at times I still have to be reminded.

Little things have value, such as breathing deeply, tasting fresh water and touching some spiritual silence.

These can provide momentary quiet from external and internal pressures.

Just knowing such peace exists helps encourage me to re-find it.

和

Happiness is tied to the straining between reality and fantasy, selfishness and selflessness, competing with others and cooperation.

Shared purpose, and our individual purpose, are they the same or opposed?

They can be in line.

The sway of reality, allows us to feel 'independence', express a quiet confidence that recognises our limitations and does not confuse subservience to an ideal with being respectful to all life.

And how important are other people, their opinions and, at times, challenging perspectives in all this?

Essential.

They're a must for us to gauge our bearings and prod us to return to practicing awareness as we navigate a course to overcome difficulties and choose to do things differently from unqueried inheritance.

Listen, truly listen to what's being said and done around us.

We all struggle with the natural strains of living and try to do 'the right thing', it's just that a little more light is required at times in our shadowed corners.

Support though can come from most unexpected quarters.

A simple smile, for instance, may be enough to change a life.

As flawed a vegan ninja as I am, with the help of others, I attempt to approach life with a question in my eye, to eternally learn, and recognise that even masters have masters.

和

忍
者

part two
recipes

drawing breath
(a brief genesis)

Vegan ninja evolve.

And no two journeys are the same.

This section of this book is about recipes, but there's more to recipes than just listing food items and setting out methods to make meals.

Recipes encompass elements of life, reflect notable ingredients of our past and choices that are interwoven with continuing procedures leading to particular and broader outcomes.

Although none of us can truly be defined by our table spread, what we do or don't eat today is indicative of influences that dance in our shadows.

Our meals also point to where we're headed.

Being vegan is immeasurably more than whether or not meat is on our menu.

Additional to a clear regard for animal welfare, life on earth, and personal health, being vegan helps in the consideration of other people, for instance, those less fortunate for a multitude of reasons.

Fair dinkum, too many of us are unaware of how our nextdoor neighbours are doing, let alone how people are fairing in a distant developing country village.

Do these sort of things matter to any of us right now?

和

Are they really part of a vegan outlook?

My answer is obvious.

Knowing a little of anyone's background can help flesh out the forces that have been exerted on them and shed light on their forward direction.

Being mindful of others enriches a holistic approach to life and our quest for meaningful balance borne of individual circumstances.

As rare as each of us think we are, interaction with others reveals remarkable differences and similarities between us all.

I was born in a small Australian country town named Singleton, in universal terms, little more than a stone's throw from my current rural abode at Elderslie, 60 years later.

A carefree, middle-class and largely uneventful upbringing ensued.

It was a charmed existence really, a child in an era of innocence when anyone could safely roam the streets from dawn to dusk in shorts, t-shirt and little on their feet.

As basic as aspects were, we were in want of nothing.

But as the eldest child in our family of eight kids, I gradually felt the gravity of expectations I was afraid I could not meet.

Wisps of rebellion arose.

They were enticed by a Catholic primary school education and public high school furthered the trend.

The yoke of conforming was a sufferance.

It became easier to drop out than apply myself.

Now and then, as a result, the difference between right and wrong was made clear to my backside by one of my dad's hobnail boots.

I had no ambition to do anything special in life, though still maintained an unrippled belief of eventually being just as successful as everyone around me.

In early teen years I began learning about trouble, nothing serious (that I'm willing to admit here), just petty larks by any self-respecting larrikin's standard.

That's when I became acquainted with disguise, playing heart-stopping tricks on adults, using crackers to blow up things such as mailboxes and how to run (fast) and hide.

As long as I turned up at home in one piece at teatime, domestic routine flowed by.

Always there'd be plenty of food, a soft bed at night and unquestionable security.

It was like coasting in life's slipstream.

In the freedom youth afforded I saw that everyone in our community was not equal, many in positions of power deserved to be challenged and while

和

the world was not fair in many respects, given a chance, the good in most ordinary people shone through adversity.

Along with a healthy defiance of authority, appreciation of my good fortune was also a seed that was sown.

These two things combined and in a limited way enabled me to oppose wrongs and help others where possible.

Rebelling had a purpose.

It wasn't all about me, it was about circumstances that needed changing and people who needed a hand.

And from the mists that are now childhood come glimpses of our family saying grace at mealtimes before taking a bite and mum doing so before every cup of tea at any hour of the day or night.

Mum's ritual endured, but the family's general blessing and expression of thanks evaporated, despite being reinforced by my school culture.

Sprouting along with five brothers and two sisters, and in the personal invulnerability of my thinking, I also took a lot for granted.

My appreciation was fairly superficial and I didn't fully understand my genuine cause for deep reflection or prayer.

Strangely though, on occasions from my late teens I would regularly catch myself assisting random people in some small way.

In instants of awareness I realised I was even pausing and quietly offering grace before occasional meals.

Then, while taking tentative steps into adulthood I developed an unusual, chronic health condition—debilitating muscular spasms in my neck that gradually twisted and shook my entire being.

Disbelief led to devastation and hospital for nine weeks where I learned a little about self-reliance and a lot about the kindness of others.

How to strive physically, mentally and spiritually came into focus.

It was evident, responsibility for me lay with me.

Yet, I was not the centre of the universe.

Although I was nobody special, others still cared.

Reflection and prayer gathered profound meaning, not merely as thoughts and words, but as something to accompany practical acts.

The significance of how I treated others, regardless of how I was treated, made sense.

I learned to look for options, not excuses.

And they weren't always in sight.

At times, even in the depths of despair, I could feel how lucky I was and could centre on people with much less than I'd previously taken for granted and those facing some sort of man-made or circumstantial calamity.

和

Although, at many a moment, my self-talk reflection was no more than a silly schoolyard ditty or slight hesitation to acknowledge my worldly surroundings, the observance of prayer through action and silent mealtime grace were becoming embedded.

Doing something for others or gratitude and consideration before eating felt natural, on a personal level, as intermittent as it was back then.

So after marrying Julie in our late 20s and beginning a family the need strengthened to say grace more often—and out loud.

At the start it remained a hit and miss affair, but it gradually took hold and now that our son and four daughters are adults, it's struck me that it's long been a regular custom we're all comfortable with.

When we come together for a meal we draw breath.

We hold hands before eating and at least one of us utters a few words of appreciation and consideration for what is set before us, those sharing the meal, those of us not present and those of us from our global family in need.

Other impromptu words, and actions, are said and done for particular individuals and particular situations as they arise.

Often these days we eat with visitors from far afield who seem to readily accept our ways and after partaking several times appear to look forward to grace.

And as un-cool as grace may be in these lightning paced, tech-savvy times it need not be so.

Whose care is it but ours, what we do or say over our meals?

So, here are a couple of mealtime examples to set you thinking, the first is for youngsters.

> *Apples and carrots, what a mix.*
> *Eat the lot and grow like sticks. Amen.*

> *Love, laughter and food shared,*
> *reminds us of times when others cared.*
> *This very moment will never return*
> *so let us be grateful of more than our*
> *plateful. Amen.*

Gratitude, it's one thing there's too little of.

And it, along with humility and patience, does not extinguish desire.

These things merely alter the way we approach life, our understanding of success and how we go about achieving.

They are oft unseen ingredients behind the best kitchen menus, subsequent discussion and action.

和

crash test dummy
(someone has to do it)

Eating.

When it comes to prominent culinary capabilities, that's probably my forte.

And it can be the most uncomplicated of things, a basic garden salad or thrown together leftovers from the fridge.

Who doesn't adore the fragrance, followed by the taste, of baked bread straight from an oven?

What about the crunchy flavour of a nutty vegetable slice, nibbling on a spicy corn fritter or savouring garlic in some warm, crisp slices of baked potato?

All unpretentious fare.

I relish minimalist 'meals', a fresh apple, drink of water and banana on the trot, for instance.

The obesity epidemic our society wallows in is the most fleshy indicator that we don't need to eat as much or as often as we too often do.

At times when I can't afford a long stop, yet munching is a must, there is nothing better than the sticky feel of juice as it dribbles down my chin while I slouch forward and slurp into a freshly cut orange.

Food enhances the moment, whether we're in the midst of a momentous occasion, knee-deep in daily work, domestic routine or tucking into the simplest of fare by ourselves out the back of nowhere.

和

Most people appreciate good food, not like swine with our snouts perpetually stuck in the trough though—in moderation.

It is the tastes, authentic tastes, both strong and subtle, that get us all in.

And that is why I have great difficulty accepting comments about vegan food being bland.

Such ill-informed criticism is a residue from days when the uninitiated saw any sort of vegetarian meal plainly as what was left on someone's plate once the meat was taken off.

In winter where I come from, that was often mashed potato, a few peas, carrots and a piece of pumpkin.

In summer it was usually a few slices of tomato, some lettuce leaves, chopped carrot and possibly two slices of tinned beetroot.

Those who have been vegan for a while know things have dramatically changed these days.

Vegans are not mugs who subsist on dull slop.

Vegan food can be a knockout.

In fact I've been tempted to do just that, knockout a few of my meat-eating mates, when they've dropped around for a barbecue.

I've been vegan so long they are past the stage of niggling me with rabbit food jokes.

Now, regardless of what's on the menu, they often expect to 'sample' so much of my food that I virtually have to beat them off with a bread stick so there's something left for me.

I may have to upgrade from such crusty weaponry.

That said, I'm neither a big eater nor a regular restaurant cuisine connoisseur.

Well, that's not quite right.

Just as it was in childhood, really I want for nothing.

Because Julie is a bit of a kitchen whiz I've customarily been treated to regular classy meals and luscious leftovers at home most of our married life.

The times of exception have usually been 'save yourself' occasions.

And despite some fairly inspired efforts, I haven't managed to poison myself.

Yet.

So, on that enticing note, let's take a stroll through the kitchen and see if my vegan world can whet your appetite.

The following recipes mainly come from Julie, our family and friends, not me.

Anything decent that is.

I've scratched a few of the basic things together, but it was Julie who has collected and, where necessary, done the experimental concocting and tweaking through the years.

I'm the crash test dummy, and an extremely lucky one at that.

和

Julie has put very few burnt offerings on our table through the years.

And I've eaten them with lashings of gratitude, knowing full well they'd probably be better than my attempt at anything similar.

Julie has managed the juggling act, meeting our day-to-day domestic demands.

She has made the household's diverse and often conflicting food requirements work.

Sometimes we've eaten completely vegan fare and other times Julie has prepared two separate meals.

Most commonly though she has adapted her menu to comply with (as she says) 'the jolly fussy vegan'.

She has provided an ingredient change here and there from outside vegan fare for those among the gathering who sought a meat, egg or cheesy option.

And another thing springs to mind before we start sorting through recipes.

I'd like to apologise to any cook I may have insulted.

When this book was in its infancy I mentioned it to a good cook at the same time as asking for her help to make a dish she felt was easy and well within even my limited capabilities.

To reduce embarrassment, I won't name the lady. (No, it wasn't Julie, although she has more than once expressed similar sentiments.)

I thought I'd asked an innocent enough question.

'Would you mind if I looked over your shoulder while you make that so I get a few more ideas for a cookbook I'm working on?'

'What?' The cook demanded in response.

I had really aggrieved her.

'That sort of thing is an insult to cooks,' the hurt one said.

'How could someone like you genuinely even contemplate writing a cookbook?'

I squirmed appropriately for a while as she held me under a steady white-hot glare.

'It's an affront to cooks to have a non-cook coming out and telling anyone what to eat and how to prepare meals,' she said.

'Cooking is about first-hand knowledge and experience working in the kitchen,' she said.

I admit it, her outburst floored me.

I'd set out to be a scribe without considering the sensitivities of real cooks.

I hadn't intended to be disrespectful or offend anyone.

But this cook made me think about what I was attempting to do.

Why was a non-cook out to create a cookbook?

Am I trying to big note myself or justify my existence?

No, I'm not aiming to take undeserved credit.

This little book is merely giving a view from the other end of a spatula.

和

It's driven by reasoning that underpins being vegan, and that I've explained in the first half of *vegan ninja*.

We have to continually cultivate a self reliance that includes a confidence to ask for help when a need surfaces.

Additionally, from a cooking perspective, what's written here is the opinion of an outsider who really would like to have a better understanding, or 'feel', for culinary culture.

I'm not pretending to be a master chef or anything of that class.

I am trying to learn the craft, attempting to be a cook who could competently back up my vegan leanings.

And now I know I could probably even survive as an unassisted cook in the kitchen, without having to resort to opening a can of baked beans at dinnertime.

I admire good cooks and I'm not attempting to speak on their behalf.

I could never be an outstanding one, even if I lived to be 100, or a smidgin older for that matter.

Great cooks are part of what's special in my life.

This book, I see as a small repayment for what has come my way, for what the cooks around me have done, especially Rupert Pitman (who's the subject of the next chapter).

I have been provided such a fantastic life.

In quieter moments I feel so undeserving because I understand I'm not entitled to a thing.

This is when my own nothingness upturns the kingdom of selfishness and I know entitlement is a delusion which belongs beyond my earthly shareholding.

Yet, so many dreams have come true.

I try to overcome the foolishness that allows realised dreams to reinflate a feeling of entitlement.

Really, the motivation behind compiling the following recipes is fairly simple.

The coming concoctions are my effort to do something constructive and practical that I hope acknowledges the creativity of 'real cooks' who have helped me.

While I aspire to be a better cook, I have no intention of treating those around me, or the fruits of their labour, as trifle.

I want to share some of the rich and random things that have come across my table, physically and figuratively, during my vegan journey so far.

Also, in my defence, I have made each of the recipes before they became part of this collection.

The only exceptions are the bulk tomato sauce and Christmas pudding, with which I have helped my principal guide—Julie on some occasions.

和

It's all been a learning curve, slow and painful many times, yet overall, rewarding.

In a way, this has allowed me to relieve an obligation I've felt to our world.

By the same token, coming to terms with cooking has not been all drudgery because overall, being vegan makes me smile, inside and out.

It would be absolutely wondrous if readers gained the same sort of sensation.

Hopefully then, *vegan ninja* is both useful in the kitchen and prompts people to continually apply their inquiring minds while building a more rooted respect for our earth's natural diversity.

So (after a few thoughts on Mr Pitman), please accept the following recipes with the regard in which they are offered.

Thank you.

和

mr pitman
(the cook)

Rupert Pitman is a legendary character, where I come from anyway.

There is an understanding within my wife Julie's family that there was not much he couldn't do.

And cook—you haven't seen or tasted anything like his fare.

Even on a bad day he could probably whip up a banquet in his morning tea break.

Well, that's the aura that enveloped Mr Pitman and still endures today, many years since his passing.

I recall that soon after Julie and I began going out together (decades ago now) she invited me to her Elderslie home for a family meal.

It was a classy country affair with silver servers, embroidered table cloths and candles for a touch of atmosphere.

Things were not long underway before Julie's younger brother, Tony, asked: 'Who cooked this?'

Julie's mum, Pam, politely finished what was in her mouth, looked briefly at Tony and said 'Mr Pitman' then resumed eating.

I didn't think much of the remark, being so nervous about meeting the family, pretending I had gentlemanly manners and trying not to spill anything.

和

Luckily everything went well.

The meal was superb, I didn't make a fool of myself and on leaving I remembered to thank Pam for her hospitality.

Several months went by before I next called into Elderslie and caught Julie and Pam in the kitchen preparing for another family meal that evening.

The place was a mess of culinary creativity and a big apple pie cooled on the bench top in the midst of it all when Tony strolled in.

'Who made the pie?' he asked.

'Who do you think?' shot Julie, 'Mr Pitman, now don't touch it.'

He didn't.

Once more, the meal that evening went well.

The food was superb, again I didn't make a fool of myself and this time I also asked for my thanks to be passed on to Mr Pitman.

That's when I was told a little about him.

He was Julie's grandfather's 'offsider', a general farmhand on the family's Elderslie and nearby Belford rural properties.

Mr Pitman was in fact the most unlikely person alive to whip up much more than fundamental save yourself tucker.

He was tall with dark hair and olive skin, a past middle-age skinny man who wore glasses, a weathered expression and well seasoned country hat.

He lived with his wife, Jean, just up the road in a timber cottage.

And to be truthful, if it wasn't for Jean, he wouldn't have even been a stick insect.

In the paddock, Mr Pitman was handy working sheep and cattle, fencing, driving tractors, digging wells, repairing buildings and growing corn and lucerne on the river flats.

While being extremely capable around the farm, in many respects Mr Pitman was ordinary.

He quietly went about his daily chores without fanfare and had a genuine 'salt of the earth', unassuming nature.

If circumstances were different perhaps he could actually have become the outstanding cook his reputation accords, but in his day men were outside toiling and women kept the home fires burning.

In a way, the social shade of Mr Pitman and his time has covered me.

During our 20s Julie and I married and continued a typical middle-class Australian tradition.

We bought a house, started a family, negotiated the bill paying treadmill, had our fair share of arguments, savoured our prosperity and kept dreaming.

For most of the first 30 years of our married life I went off to work in the city while Julie

和

coordinated the domestic scene, doing the lion's share of child rearing and, of course, the cooking.

Mr Pitman's name popped up many, many times.

Like I said, boy could he cook!

Our five adult children could probably still refer to 'his' finer efforts.

Years coasted by like clouds.

We moved to live permanently at Elderslie and in 2005 Julie and I were involved in the first of several farmer's markets at our little community village hall.

We decided to run a food stall, a vegan stall with several varieties of savouries and sweets, to raise money for charity.

Julie was not keen on being the central attraction in our effort, and as I was the jolly vegan, we settled on the name *Paul's Pies* for our little venture.

At each of the following markets, all but one of our stalls was a complete sell-out.

And even that one was pretty close.

Most Elderslie locals know Julie is a good cook and despite telling our stall customers that I was merely the vegetable masher, apple peeler and washing-upper it appears some people believed I was being more than slightly modest.

Perhaps they thought that if I was vegan I'd have to be a great cook, or else I'd die.

They were partly right.

I was vegan and someone in our household had to be a good cook or I would die.

(Thank heavens for Julie.)

'Sometimes truth is much more difficult to sell than a date muffin,' I told one admirer.

Recently Julie and I went to another function at the hall and as we carried in plates of her slices, cakes and savouries to share with others for supper I received a few glowing comments on my cooking from people who live in the adjoining valley.

'Thanks, but really it's Julie, not me,' I unsuccessfully protested.

They knowingly smiled back and made some cute dismissive comment.

I let it pass.

Yes, these days I do have a bit of a go in the kitchen, but I struggle and can't see a moment when my culinary efforts will match Julie's.

So, I think next time a cooking compliment wafts my way I'll have to deflect it harder, perhaps boot it right out into the paddock towards someone eminently more deserving, like Mr Pitman.

和

from little things
(all hinges on starting)

Big things grow from the smallest kernel, so a few culinary basics must be planted to continue.

It's not that I think *vegan ninja* readers are dummies, it's just that when I've been under instruction some of my mentors have assumed certain things were so obvious they didn't need explanation.

In fact, many 'obvious' things are still far from that for me.

So, I'd like what follows to be of use to my soul mates, other cookery battlers, even if it does raise a giggle among more experienced cooks.

The trick to being a good cook lies in being organised.

Read your recipes before striking a blow.

Plan ahead and buy what's needed in advance.

If a few days pass between shopping and making a particular dish, check that someone in the household hasn't eaten any necessary ingredient.

Accept you may have to substitute one ingredient for another if you haven't everything at your fingertips.

Using accurate measuring cups and spoons is a good habit.

Any old mug or spoon in a top drawer can really throw out the end result of what you're making.

Experience is the best guide. A little extra corn in the fritters won't hurt, whereas a hefty dose of chilli might.

和

I assemble ingredients on the bench and do as much peeling and chopping of things as possible before getting underway.

I refer to the recipe as I go, use a timer where necessary and try to be ready for each next step well before I need to take it.

If you can reuse a bowl, cup or spoon for a later step give them a quick rinse and do so.

Try and keep your work area clean and orderly and be aware of hot pots and pans and sharp knives.

Time permitting, rinse boards, knives and other items as you finish with them to speed up the eventual job.

It's amazing how much washing-up a meal can generate.

To reduce waste, make sure airtight containers for leftover bits and pieces actually are airtight and infrequently used ingredients are bought in small quantities.

Fresh foods are best so if there is a chance of growing your own vegetables, or herbs in pots, have a go.

Although our home-grown efforts have been up and down through the years, the tomatoes from our best-ever crop last summer proved there's nothing more tasty or pleasing than eating produce from your own garden and giving away the surplus.

Sprouting beans and seeds is also worth the effort.

It doesn't take much time, or space, and the germination process increases vitamin C substantially and makes it easier for us to digest things like the grain's iron, calcium and many other elements.

Mushrooms provide some vitamin B12 and essential minerals such as selenium, potassium and phosphorus.

Big flat ones are more flavoursome than small ones, and if you put them out in the sun for an hour or so before you eat them their vitamin D level increases dramatically.

Rice is a basic, versatile food that's worth knowing how to cook and include in healthy, balanced eating.

Short-grain is starchy and cooks soft and sticky.

Long-grain is less starchy so remains more separated.

Although white rice loses many nutrients through processing, its benefits still include carbohydrates to quickly boost our energy and amino acids to promote muscle growth.

Brown, black, red and wild rice don't store as long, and take longer than white rice to cook, but are richer in proteins, fibre, vitamins and minerals.

Try not to overcook vegetables.

They look and taste better if they're on the crisp side of cooked, rather than the mushy side.

和

When cooking in water, bring it to the boil first and then add your vegies or pasta.

This gives you a more accurate cooking time and helps to seal in the nutrients.

Be mindful of sugar and salt use and try to cut them back.

Have fruit in a bowl in your eating area.

You'll see and smell when it's ripe.

Our 'children' still reach for fruit when they walk in and commercial confectionary doesn't rate a look (not too often anyway).

Nuts are also handy to have about, mainly for the same reason.

And like fruit, they're versatile and packed with goodness.

Big, sharp knives and big chopping boards are safer and more efficient than little ones, particularly when preparing meals for several people or when dealing with tougher vegetables such as pumpkins. (Although I have a favourite little knife and cute bamboo board I usually can't reach past, especially when there's just a few of us at home.)

And to complete the basics, here are a few uncomplicated edibles that could repeatedly prove to be very handy.

和

steamed white rice (absorption cooking method)

1 cup of rice
1 ½ cups of water

Give the rice a quick rinse then put it and the water in a saucepan. Stir rice to evenly distribute the grains, put lid on, bring water to the boil then turn the heat down to a simmer for 10 minutes and turn off. Allowing it to then steam for a while, with the lid on and the heat off, seems to add to the rice's fluffiness.

If you check the rice after 10 minutes cooking and the water is not quite absorbed you can continue simmering for two more minutes or allow water to be absorbed by letting it sit steaming for ten minutes. If the water is absorbed, but rice is still a little hard, add a small amount of water and simmer for a few more minutes. Fluff the rice with a fork before serving.

Serves 3.

This may be simple, but the method works well to produce light, fluffy results. Rice can be used in so many dishes. Keep the rice/water ratio the same to serve more people.

wholegrain brown rice

Wholegrain brown rice is cooked the same way, except it takes longer—30 minutes of simmering after it's come to the boil.

和

asparagus (blanched)

1 bunch of asparagus

Cut a centimetre or so off the bottom of the stalks (as this piece can be a bit woody when bought from a shop) then cut the stalks in half so they are 10 centimetres or so long.

Put enough water in a saucepan to just cover the bunch and bring it to the boil. Now pop the asparagus in the water, bring it back to the boil and leave the asparagus there for about 30 seconds. Turn off the heat, drain the water and eat the asparagus as soon as possible.

As a light bite by itself, I find a plate of asparagus an absolute treat. Usually though it's eaten with a meal so, in that case, leave its cooking right to last so it's warm with the rest of the dish.

It's great if you grow your own, but if you buy it from a shop, eat it as soon as you can to maximise the freshness. Asparagus dries out from the bottom, so the longer you leave it in the fridge the more woodiness you should cut off the stem's base.

和

garden salad

¼ lettuce
2 tomatoes
½ purple onion
2 carrots

Bunch the lettuce together and slice it every centimetre or two and pop it into a serving bowl. Cut the tomatoes in half then each half into quarters and put them in the bowl. Slice the onion fairly finely and throw it in. Purple onions look interesting and have a milder taste than some other onions. If you prefer a more onion tasting salad use a whole one, or stronger tasting one and don't cut it too small. Wash the carrots and slice them in half, top to toe, and then through the middle. Now carefully cut them lengthways so they're like big matchsticks. Put them in, mix everything and serve.

Serves 2.

It's simple, goes together in a jiffy and is rarely out of place. If you have a bit more time, or want something more elaborate, throw in other ingredients such as chopped beetroot, capsicum, cashews, almonds or other nuts, a little sliced pineapple or avocado.

和

hope's hash browns

3 medium potatoes
¼ cup of vegetable oil
pinch of pepper

Peel, wash and grate the potatoes into a bowl and mix in the pepper. Squeeze excess water out of the mixture. You don't want it sitting in water. You want it moist enough to stick together yet fairly dry so your patties will go crisp. Use the mixture immediately as it will go grey and lose moisture the longer it is left unused.

Lightly cover the bottom of a frying pan with oil and heat it. Using a tablespoon, scoop the grated potato into patties, about 4cm across and 1cm, or less, thick. Cook each side golden brown then place them on paper to absorb excess oil before quickly serving.

Serves 4.

Youngsters of all ages enjoy this speedy snack. Alongside a basic salad they provide an x-factor to something nutritional that's too often overlooked by some people as boring.

和

apple fritters

2 cups self-raising flour
4 medium green apples
a few teaspoons of vegetable oil

Gradually add water to the flour and stir it into a thick but runny batter. Peel, core and thinly slice the apples and add them to the batter, making sure they are well covered.

Put a light film of oil in a frypan and heat it. Using a tablespoon as a rough measure, spoon your mixture into the hot pan, patting each fritter down to about 1cm high. When they bubble on top a little they're ready to flip to cook the other side. After taking the first few out, add some more oil before the next ones go in. If time allows, place them on paper as you take them from the pan to soak up the oil.

Serves 4.

These fritters are quick and easy. They are great hot with soy ice cream and a leftover treat during the next few days, if they ever last that long.

和

Keeping things simple is a recipe for life generally.

I start the day with a hearty breakfast cereal, use as many uncooked greens (spinach leaves, bok choy and other Asian vegetables) in other meals as I can, keep as active as possible and reach for drinking water before, and usually to the exclusion of anything else.

Breathing deeply, trying not to overeat, and resting for physical and mental recovery, are also essential to my routine.

Simplicity in dietary terms is also the best way to go.

We can't beat fresh fruit and vegetables, in fact numerous studies show that some everyday fruit and vegetables found in supermarkets are just as good for us as more expensive, exotic items the media has tagged 'superfoods'.

For example, ordinary old apples, oranges, melons, carrots, broccoli, parsley, spinach, lettuce, olive oil (for cooking) and nuts contain antioxidants, have essential nutrients and vitamins and help reduce numerous general health and cancer risks.

And, one last thought on recipes.

They are fundamentally guides to feed our creativity.

Experiment.

If there are particular ingredients you're not keen on, change them, and alter quantities to suit your tastes.

和

breakfasts and smoothies

andean rice

4 cups of wholegrain brown rice
6 cups of water
2 cups of sultanas
1 cup of red quinoa (pronounced keen-whah)

Rince the rice then pop all ingredients into a big saucepan and stir them together to evenly distribute and break up air bubbles.

With the lid on, bring to the boil, then turn it down to a simmer for 30 minutes.

Turn off heat and allow to cool with the lid on as the steam will keep it cooking for a while.

Makes enough for one person for a week or two.

I keep it in a sealed container in the fridge and re-heat some with soy milk in a small saucepan and either use it on top of my breakfast muesli or put it in a container with chopped banana, apple or pear and take it with me as a treat through the day.

和

banana smoothie

1 litre of soy milk
2 bananas
½ granny smith apple
1 nutmeg
1 ½ cups of soy ice cream

Pour the soy milk into a blender, grind the nutmeg on top and, using a tablespoon, scoop in some of the soy ice cream. Give the blender a whirl when you have a few ice cream spoonfuls in as it's easier for the blender to handle a gradual load.

Cut the apple into about 2cm pieces, leaving the skin on. Pop them into the blender and give it another whirl.

Peel the bananas, break them into three or four pieces and gradually add and blend them.

That's it. Enjoy.

Makes 6 good sized drinks.

和

bircher muesli

750 grams of rolled oats
125 grams of linseeds (flaxseeds)
150 grams of sunflower seeds
100 grams of pumpkin seeds
100 grams of dried apricots, roughly chopped
125 grams of dates, roughly chopped
200 grams of brazil nuts, roughly chopped
½ cup of shredded coconut

This is a version of muesli created by Swiss dietitian Dr Maximilian Bircher in 1887.

Use any combination of nuts and dried fruit you prefer (such as cranberries or sultanas).

Combine all ingredients in a large container.

Put as much as you'd like for breakfast in a bowl and add enough water (or soy milk) to just cover it.

Leave it in the fridge to soak overnight then in the morning add fresh fruit, extra soy milk or water as desired.

Soaked grains and nuts are easier to digest and your body is more able to take in their nutrients.

Store remaining muesli in an airtight container in the pantry.

Makes enough to last one person a few weeks.

和

celery and apple smoothie

2 cups of water
3 large celery stalks
2 green (granny smith) apples
2 bananas
1 tablespoon of ground linseed (flaxseed)
1 lime

This smoothie is thick.

Cut the tough foot off the celery and discard. Rinse the remainder then trim off the leaves and chop them a bit as you cut the stalks into 2cm to 3cm lengths. Leave skin on apples, cut them into quarters, core and cut each quarter into four pieces. Skin the bananas and break them into three pieces.

Pour the water into a kitchen blender and add a small handful of celery. Blend well then add the rest of the ingredients gradually. Blend them by the handful so you don't overload the machine. Add juice of the lime at the end.

Celery can be hard work for the blender so it is better to get it in first. Clean the blender immediately because the job will be easier before the residue turns to crust that is hard to remove. If you can't drink it all straight away it will last a day or so in the fridge but will need a stir.

Fills about 6 brimming cups.

和

dragon's muesli

750 grams of rolled oats
juice of 4 oranges
190 grams of sunflower seeds
250 grams of shredded coconut
380 grams of natural almonds, roughly chopped
100 grams of sweetened, dried cranberries
500 grams of sultanas
200 grams of dried apricots, chopped to about sultana size
100 grams of pepita seeds

This breakfast cereal takes its name from a term of endearment bestowed on Julie by one of my old mates and the fact that oats used in the recipe are roasted.

Using a large basin, pour orange juice over the oats and mix thoroughly to coat as much of the oats as possible.

Then spread the oats evenly on large oven trays and bake at 160 degrees until they are golden brown. Keep an eye on them and stir occasionally to prevent burning.

When cooked, mix in all the other ingredients and store the muesli in an air tight container in the pantry.

Julie prefers the smaller pieces, rather than say the whole almonds in ninja muesli, because you get a better mix of tastes in each spoonful.

It also has a crisper texture than if raw oats were used.

Sometimes ground linseed is added to the mix.

With each breakfast bowl, Julie slices in half an apple and half a banana and tops the muesli with soy milk.

Makes enough to last one person about a fortnight.

This muesli is a much more crunchy cereal than ninja muesli.

和

ninja muesli

170 gram packet of puffed millet
170 gram packet of puffed kamut
(puffed rice and puffed wheat also do the trick as alternatives)
750 grams of almonds, leave whole or chop if you wish
500 grams of sultanas
150 grams of shredded, diced or desiccated coconut
200 grams of uncrystallised naked ginger
200 grams of sesame seeds
200 grams of sunflower seeds
200 grams of pepitas (pumpkin seeds)
500 grams of rolled oats

Chop the ginger into small pieces so it adds interest, rather than an overpowering taste. Mix all the ingredients by hand in two big plastic tubs, then put what you can into two good sized air-tight glass jars for use at the table. The tubs, with lids, are used to store what won't fit in the jars.

The second jar is really only for my peace of mind. It allows me a week's grace before I have to go to town to get more and it also ensures enough is on hand to cater for a full house of blow-in guests.

I put a hefty serving of ninja muesli on three wheat biscuits, drown the lot in soy milk and slice fresh seasonal fruit on top. Most mornings that includes an apple cut into little pieces and with the skin left on. This week will also include bananas and peaches. Next week pears, rockmelon or some other fruit may be better priced so they will top off breakfast.

A sprinkling of ground linseed (also known as flaxseed), can add a nice touch to the meal. Time permitting, I buy flaxseeds then blend up about half a cupful to sprinkle a dessertspoon full over breakfast.

和

The blended amount lasts several days and keeps fresh in the fridge.

Don't worry about being exact with quantities or precise with ingredients you use in the ninja muesli mix.

Regularly I throw in a 900 gram packet of rolled oats, different nuts, currants and raisins, instead of other ingredients, puffed rice rather than millet, for instance. Supermarket prices and ingredient availability dictate what goes in.

I find organic puffed grains taste best. There are commonly available brands that are not genetically modified and have no added salt, sugar or artificial flavours and colours.

A 250 gram packet of quinoa (pronounced keen-whah) flakes or organic puffed quinoa can also add interest but it's an occasional treat as it's not cheap. Quinoa, also known as 'the mother grain', is rich in proteins and high in fibre.

Sultanas, naturally dried and without preservatives, also taste better than those with more chemical input.

Makes enough to last one person a month or so.

I reckon there is no better way to begin the day than with a good drink of fresh water followed by ninja muesli. That's my staple morning starter. I usually eat it with three wheat biscuits and a generous helping of fresh fruit. It travels well and tastes great even with water if you don't have soy milk handy. I ate it regularly with water for a long time until I was softened by the convenience and taste of soy milk.

和

kale smoothie

½ a bunch of kale
2 cups of water
2 medium bananas
juice of ½ a lime

Strip the leaves from the stalk pop the leaves into a blender along with the water, bananas and lime juice. (Throw the kale stalk into the compost bin.)

Flick the blender on and blend until the ingredients are smooth. Simple.

Makes enough to fill about four 300 millilitre bottles.

It lasts several days in the fridge so you can take a bottle or two to work throughout the week. As the smoothie settles you have to give the bottles a good shake before drinking. You could spice it up by adding mint, ginger or something else to your liking.

和

quinoa sunrise
(pronounced keen—whah)

1 cup of red quinoa
1 ½ cups of water
1 ½ cups of almonds, finely chopped
2 apples, skin on and finely chopped
2 bananas, finely chopped
2 tablespoons of ground linseed

Rinse the quinoa, put it in a saucepan with the water, bring to the boil and with the lid on, turn down heat to simmer for 10 minutes. It should absorb the water. I like red quinoa just for the colour it adds to meals.

Chop the fruit and nuts as the quinoa is cooking.

While hot, place a serving of quinoa in a breakfast bowl with cold soy milk then sprinkle on the linseed, apple, banana and nuts.

Serves 4 people.

If all the cooked quinoa isn't eaten, pop it in the fridge for a leftover breakfast the next day. You can eat it cold with soy milk and freshly chopped fruit and nuts but it's a nice treat warmed up.

Put the quinoa in a saucepan, tip in enough soy milk so it's almost covered and gently heat it through before placing it in your bowl with fruit and nuts. For a little more sweetness, add a desert spoon of sultanas when warming the quinoa.

和

mains and soups

borscht

4 medium to large beetroots, peeled and chopped
¼ savoy cabbage, chopped
1 onion, chopped
2 celery sticks, chopped
1 medium carrot, peeled and chopped
1 parsnip, peeled and chopped
2 tablespoons of parsley, chopped
a good splash of red wine vinegar
¾ cup of tomato puree
2 garlic cloves, crushed
2 teaspoons of vegetable stock
2 cups of water
salt and pepper to season
8 baby potatoes, peeled and quartered
1 tablespoon of chopped fresh chives

Place everything in the ingredients list above the potatoes into a large stockpot. Add just enough water to cover. With lid on, bring to the boil and cook for about 25 minutes, until tender. Blend and check seasoning.

While soup is cooking, boil potatoes until tender but not soft. The meal is better when you have something to sink your teeth into.

To serve, put four potato quarters into each bowl, pour in the soup and top with fresh chives.

Serves 8.

This hearty dish has the flavour to match its rich Russian colouring. Nice one Igor.

和

broccoli and basil soup

1 medium onion, chopped
2 garlic cloves, chopped
1 large head of broccoli (or two bunches of broccolini)
½ a cup of fresh basil leaves
6 cups of vegetable stock
1 tablespoon of vegetable oil
salt and pepper (to taste)

Heat oil in a large saucepan, add the onion and garlic and saute until soft and lightly brown. Add roughly chopped broccoli and stock. Bring to the boil with lid on then turn down to simmer until greens are just cooked.

Don't overcook them as you want them slightly firm for the texture, colour and better taste.

Using a blender (or potato masher if you like your soup chunky) blend soup with the fresh basil leaves then add salt and pepper to taste.

Serves 4 to 6.

和

carrot and ginger (or tomato and ginger) soup

1 medium onion, chopped
2cm of fresh ginger, chopped
5 medium carrots (or 2 tins of tomatoes, juice and all)
½ a red capsicum, chopped
6 cups of vegetable stock (or 3 cups for tomato version)
dash of sesame oil
1 tablespoon of vegetable oil
salt and pepper (to taste)
handful of chopped parsley for garnish

Heat oil in a large saucepan, add onion and ginger and sauté until soft and lightly brown. Add roughly chopped carrots (or tinned tomatoes), capsicum and stock. Bring to the boil with lid on then turn down to simmer until carrots are just cooked.

Using a blender, blend until smooth. Add salt, pepper and sesame oil to taste, serve into bowls and garnish with parsley.

Serves 4 to 6.

和

cassoulet

2 cups of dried lima beans
1 tablespoon of vegetable oil
1 medium onion, finely chopped
3 medium carrots, sliced into coins
2 medium tomatoes, roughly chopped
1 head of broccoli, cut into little trees
½ a head of cauliflower, cut into little trees
2 teaspoons of fresh oregano, finely chopped
½ teaspoon salt
freshly ground black pepper to taste
2 teaspoons of vegetable stock

Put washed beans in a saucepan and add six cups of water. Bring to the boil, boil for two minutes then remove from the heat. Cover and leave in the water for one hour. Drain and put aside.

Heat oil in a pan and add the onion, carrot and tomatoes and fry until the onion is transparent. Add the oregano, salt, pepper, vegetable stock, three and a half cups of water and the drained beans. Bring to the boil and simmer with the saucepan lid off for one hour or until beans are tender. Put in the cauliflower and broccoli right at the end of the process and simmer for five minutes until they are just cooked. You want the cauliflower and broccoli only lightly cooked so they add a texture rather than mush to the dish. Serve with crusty bread.

A quicker method is to soak the beans in water for about eight hours or overnight if it is convenient. This allows you to do away with the initial boiling. It will also shorten the simmering time down to about half an hour before the beans are tender.

Serves 6.

和

curried parsnip soup

1 teaspoon of cumin seeds
2 teaspoons of coriander seeds
1 tablespoon of vegetable oil
1 onion, peeled and chopped
1 garlic clove, crushed
½ teaspoon of ground turmeric
¼ teaspoon of chilli powder
1 cinnamon quill
450 grams of parsnips, peeled and chopped
1 litre of vegetable stock
salt and pepper
handful of fresh coriander, finely chopped

Using a small frypan, dry fry cumin and coriander seeds over a moderate heat for about two minutes, stirring until lightly toasted. Reserve until cooled then grind in a mortar and pestle. Heat oil in a saucepan. Cook onion until soft and golden, keeping it moving to prevent burning. Add turmeric, chilli powder and cinnamon quill and cook for one minute.

Add parsnips and stir well. Put in the ground cumin, coriander and salt and pepper to taste. Pour in the stock and bring to the boil. Cover and simmer for 15 minutes or until parsnips are cooked.

Allow soup to cool. As the cinnamon quill was only used for flavouring, remove and discard it. Blend the soup until very smooth, reheat gently and season to taste if necessary. Serve and garnish with the fresh coriander.

Serves 4.

This is a spice lovers soup. It goes down well with a little bread.

和

falafel

2 x 400 gram tins of chickpeas
(or 225 grams of dried chickpeas)
1 onion, very finely chopped
1 garlic clove, crushed
3 slices of bread, processed to crumbs
¼ teaspoon of chilli powder
1 teaspoon of coriander, ground
1 teaspoon of cumin, ground
2 tablespoons of parsley, finely chopped,
salt and pepper
vegetable oil for frying

If using dried chickpeas, soak them overnight in plenty of water. Drain and rinse then cover them with plenty of fresh water in a large saucepan and cook for one to one and a half hours until tender. Drain them again.

Using a food processor, chop the chickpeas to a dry, fairly even consistency and put them into a large mixing bowl.

To the processed chickpeas, add the fresh breadcrumbs and remaining ingredients. Now add just enough water to form a slightly moist but stiff mixture by mixing them well for a few minutes.

Let mixture rest for one to two hours. Falafel patties are firmer if the mixture is allowed to chill in a fridge for a few hours or overnight.

Form the mixture into small patties and shallow fry in hot vegetable oil.

Makes enough for 4 people.

These are yummy served hot with lemon wedges and salad and great as a cold alternative to vegie burgers as a staple for salad sandwich lunches.

和

family spinach parcels

1 bunch of spinach, rinsed and roughly chopped
200 grams of mushrooms, sliced
1 cup of thick white sauce (see page 246)
½ cup of walnuts or mixed nuts, chopped
½ a red capsicum
1 small onion, finely chopped
½ cup of sesame seeds
4 sheets of vegan puffed pastry

Cook onion and capsicum until onion is lightly browned (sautéd) and set aside. Place spinach in a large saucepan with half a cup of water. Put lid on and bring to the boil, reduce heat and simmer for four minutes. Drain and return to the saucepan. Add onion, capsicum, mushrooms and white sauce to the spinach and combine well.

Pre-heat oven to 200 degrees.

Thaw pastry sheets. Spoon the mixture into the centre of each sheet leaving a few centimetres around the edges to fold over. Begin by folding the front of the pastry about halfway over the top. Fold the sides in and then bring the back over towards you so it encloses the mixture in a parcel.

Spray or brush each parcel with water and sprinkle them with sesame seeds. Place parcels in the oven until golden and puffed. They should take about 15 minutes. Keep an eye on them so the pastry doesn't burn.

Each parcel serves 2 (or one burly footballer).

These parcels are a meal in themselves, but are something special if eaten with mashed potato, boiled carrots and broccoli. They last a few days in the fridge and also freeze well.

和

family pizza

dough

>   *2 cups of warm water*
>   *7 gram sachet of dried yeast*
>   *5 cups of plain flour*

topping

>   *1 tablespoon of vegetable oil*
>   *½ a brown onion, finely chopped*
>   *3 garlic cloves, crushed*
>   *400 gram tin of tomatoes*
>   *½ to 1 red capsicum, finely chopped*
>   *½ to 1 red onion, chopped*
>   *1 cup of cooked, chopped spinach*
>   *3 cups of roasted pumpkin pieces*
>   *8 large, flat mushrooms (or 20 small ones)*
>   *handful of raw cashews*
>   *salt and pepper to taste*

In a large bowl combine the warm water and dried yeast. Allow the dough
   mixture to sit for 10 to 15 minutes then add four of the five cups of flour
   and mix to a stiff batter.

Keep the extra cup of flour aside.

Cover the bowl with plastic wrap or transfer the mixture into a large lidded
   container and leave the dough to double in size (overnight or for a few
   hours during the day).

When ready to cook, preheat the oven to 200 degrees, remove the lid or
   plastic wrap and gradually mix in the extra flour then knead the dough
   on a floured bench top until smooth.

After kneading, let the base rest for a few minutes.

Then divide the dough roughly in half and press each half into its own oiled

和

oven tray to about half a centimetre thick and set aside while you prepare the topping.

Make the tomato sauce by heating the tablespoon of vegetable oil in a small saucepan and sautéing the brown onion and crushed garlic until soft.

Mash the tinned tomatoes and add them along with salt and pepper, to taste.

Mix it all well and simmer for five to 10 minutes.

While this is cooking, prepare the remaining topping ingredients. Don't cut the onion too thinly or it will just burn and shrivel up. Cut the mushrooms into thirds and the pumpkin into about one to two centimetre pieces. (The roasted pumpkin and cooked spinach can be leftovers from a previous meal or cooked in the 15 minutes you let the dough sit when starting the pizza.)

When topping ingredients are ready, spread the tomato sauce over the two pizza bases (any left over can be frozen for another pizza day).

Now sprinkle the chopped capsicum, red onion, spinach, pumpkin pieces, cut mushrooms and cashews evenly over the bases.

Bake in the over at 200 degrees for about 15 to 20 minutes, until golden. Enjoy.

Pizzas can be a smorgasbord of tastes by replacing some of the above ingredients with alternatives or using leftovers in the topping.

For example, boiled potato, boiled sweet potato or cooked tofu, pineapple or tomato cut into one to two centimetre pieces.

Pieces of broccoli or green leaves, such as spinach, can also be added but to prevent them being burned to a crisp, bury them under more robust ingredients such as pumpkin, tomato, mushroom or capsicum.

Serves 6.

和

firey butternut pumpkin and tomato soup

1 butternut pumpkin
1 large onion, peeled, roughly chopped
2 large garlic cloves, peeled roughly chopped
1 teaspoon of finely chopped fresh chilli
(or chilli paste, such as sambal oeleck)
2 teaspoons of powdered vegetable stock
(or 2 vegetable stock cubes)
1 tablespoon of vegetable oil
4 tomatoes, skinned, roughly chopped
salt and pepper
1 tablespoon of fresh coriander, chopped

Peel the butternut, remove seeds and chop into 3cm chunks.

Heat oil in a large saucepan, add the onion and garlic and sauté until the onion softens. Add chopped chilli, or chilli paste, cook for one minute and keep stirred to prevent burning.

Add pumpkin and tomato pieces and enough water to not quite cover the vegetables. Stir in the stock powder, put the lid on and bring to the boil. Simmer for 25 minutes or until vegetables are soft.

Using a blender, or food processor, blend the vegetables and stock until smooth. Return to the saucepan, add salt and pepper to taste, add chopped tomatoes and simmer for 10 minutes. Stir in the coriander at the end and serve with crusty bread.

Serves 6.

If you want to tame it, halve the chilli.

和

fragrant tofu curry

1 purple onion, finely chopped
2 tablespoons of fresh ginger, grated
2 garlic cloves, crushed
2 tablespoons of olive oil
2 tablespoons of curry powder
½ tablespoon of ground turmeric
1 cinnamon stick
500 grams of tomatoes, diced
350 gram block of firm tofu
⅓ cup of red lentils
1 ½ cups of frozen peas
2 tablespoons of coriander, chopped
2 cups of water

Cut the tofu into 1cm to 2cm cubes and set aside.

Mix the onion, ginger and garlic well together. (You could use a food processor or stick blender to process them into a paste if you preferred a smoother texture.) Heat the oil in a deep-sided iron saucepan and cook the onion, ginger and garlic for two minutes. Add the spices and cook for another minute. Keep stirred to prevent burning. Add the water and tomatoes and bring to the boil. Now add the tofu, lentils, cinnamon and peas, bring back to the boil then simmer for 15 minutes or until the lentils are soft. Discard the cinnamon stick, stir in the coriander and serve.

Serves 6.

This spicy dish goes well with steamed rice, potato, a Chinese noodle salad or steamed greens to compliment the flavour and texture.

和

fresh spring rolls

1 cup of rice vermicelli noodles
1 teaspoon of sesame oil
1 large garlic clove, crushed
1red chilli, seeded and finely chopped
1 teaspoon of sugar
juice of 1 lime (or lemon)
1 large carrot, peeled and grated
1 cup of bean sprouts, chopped roughly
½ cup of chopped, fresh coriander
½ cup of chopped fresh mint
½ cup of roasted, unsalted peanuts, chopped
black pepper to taste
rice paper, 170cm square

dipping sauce
3 tablespoons of tamari soy sauce
3 tablespoons of mirin
1 teaspoon of sesame seed oil

Soak noodles in a bowl of boiling water for five minutes or until soft.

Meanwhile, heat sesame oil and sauté garlic and chilli for two minutes. Add sugar and lime juice to a pan and stir well. Drain noodles and rinse in cold water to remove any sticky starch.

Cut noodles into 2cm or 3cm lengths. Mix garlic and chilli through noodles then add other vegetables, herbs and nuts. Combine well and season with pepper.

To make the rolls, dip each sheet of rice paper into hot water and then lay a softened sheet onto the workbench and spoon a small amount of noodle salad about one third of the way up the sheet, leaving room on the sides for folding. It is best to fold sheets diagonally.

和

Lift the front of the sheet over the mixture, tuck in the sides and tightly roll the remaining paper around the parcel.

Make the dipping sauce by combining the soy sauce, mirim and sesame seed oil then serve.

Makes about 20.

The dipping sauce gives these rolls flavour. I love their fresh nature and tend to skip a dip into the sauce occasionally to savour their rawness. They have a damp feel in your fingers and the subtle taste may not be strong enough for people used to traditional hot spring rolls.

和

ginger, butternut and lentil soup

4cm knob of fresh ginger, chopped
2 cups of butternut pumpkin, cut roughly into about 2cm cubes
1 medium onion, chopped
2 cups of vegetable stock
1 x 400 gram tin of tomatoes or three fresh ones, roughly chopped
½ a cup of red lentils
1 tablespoon of vegetable oil
salt and pepper to taste

Place oil in a large saucepan, heat and sauté the onions. Add pumpkin and
    sauté a little longer, then add the remaining ingredients.
Bring to the boil, reduce heat to a simmer and cook until pumpkin is soft.
    Stir occasionally and check that the lentils aren't catching on the bottom.
Once cooked, either mash or pop it in a blender and process.

Serves 2 to 3.

和

grace's spanish lentejas

2 cups of green or brown lentils, rinsed, soaked overnight and drained
1 large onion, finely diced
1 green capsicum, diced
1 large potato, peeled and diced
2 medium carrots, peeled and diced
3 garlic cloves, crushed
2 tablespoons of chopped parsley
3 dried bay leaves
1 teaspoon of ground paprika
salt and pepper, to taste
1 tablespoon of olive oil

Heat the oil in a large heavy frypan and add the onion, garlic, paprika, diced vegetables, parsley, lentils, salt and pepper. Saute lightly then add just enough water to prevent lentils from burning. Put lid on and simmer, stirring occasionally, until lentils and vegetables are cooked. Add extra water if needed to prevent burning.

Serve with bread and salad.

Serves 4.

和

hope's pumpkin and pea soup

½ a large kent pumpkin
2 tablespoons of vegetable oil
1 large onion, roughly chopped
2 large garlic cloves, roughly chopped
1 dessertspoon of powdered vegetable stock
2 potatoes
3 cups of frozen peas
salt and pepper, to taste

Peel the pumpkin, remove seeds and chop into 3cm to 4cm chunks. Peel the potatoes and chop into chunks slightly smaller than the pumpkin as potato generally takes a little longer to cook than pumpkin pieces the same size.

Heat oil in a large saucepan, or boiler. Add onion and garlic and sauté until soft, stirring occasionally. Add pumpkin and potato pieces and enough water to barely cover the vegetables. Add powder stock, salt and pepper. Bring to the boil with lid on.

Reduce heat to a simmer and cook for about 30 minutes or until vegetables are soft. Allow the vegetables and stock to cool for 10 minutes or so then blend until smooth. Be careful, the hot liquid can pop the blender's lid. Use a tea towel and hold the lid on. Only fill the blender to about 40 per cent.

Pour the blend into a container and when blending completed return it to the saucepan. Add the peas, salt and pepper to taste and briefly bring the soup to the boil to cook the peas. It's now ready to serve.

Makes 4 litres.

This soup freezes well and makes for a very light and easy meal when you don't feel like cooking. It's a great basic recipe that you can do a lot with, depending on what you have at hand. For example, instead of peas,

和

feel free to use broccoli, fresh corn (cut off the cob) or sliced carrots for instance or add one teaspoon of finely chopped fresh ginger as well as the garlic for extra flavour.

和

lentils and rice

2 tablespoons of vegetable oil
2 onions, finely chopped
2 garlic cloves, crushed
1 tablespoon of ground cumin
2 teaspoons of ground coriander
1 cup of brown or green lentils, rinsed and drained
1 cup of brown rice
1 litre of vegetable stock
2 carrots, peeled
2 tomatoes
2 potatoes, peeled
1 broccoli head
1 teaspoon of salt
1 red capsicum, sliced
2 cups of baby spinach leaves
lavash bread

Soak lentils in plenty of water for six or so hours, say over night or in the morning for that evening's meal. Drain and rinse before use.

Chop the carrots, tomatoes, potatoes and broccoli into bite-sized pieces.

Heat oil in a large pan. Add onion and cook over medium heat for 10 minutes or until browned. Add the garlic and spices and stir-fry for one minute.

Add the stock, lentils, rice, carrots, tomatoes and potatoes and bring to the boil.

Reduce heat as low as possible and simmer for one hour. During the last 10 minutes check the mixture isn't sticking to the bottom and add the broccoli and salt.

The lentils and rice should be tender and stock completely absorbed, if

和

not keep cooking and keep an eye on it.

When ready to serve, add sliced capsicum and spinach leaves then serve with lavash bread.

Serves 6.

This was the first meal I ever cooked from a recipe and three of the four people at the table finished everything that was on their plates that evening. It was a roaring success.

(No, the fourth didn't keel over, they'd eaten just prior and weren't hungry.)

和

japanese soba stir-fry

2½ cm of fresh ginger, finely chopped
1 tablespoon of sesame oil
3 carrots, peeled, finely chopped into coins
1 large broccoli head, cut into flowerettes
½ red capsicum, finely chopped
1 bunch of choy sum (or bok choy), chop into 2cm lengths
1 tablespoon of seasame seeds
½ cup of dry, roasted almonds
2 tablespoons of tamari soy sauce
2 tablespoons of mirin
270 gram packet of organic soba noodles

Heat sesame oil in a large pan or wok. Add the ginger and stir-fry for one minute, taking care not to burn it. Add all the prepared vegetables and stir-fry for three or four minutes then take off the heat. You want the vegetables still crisp.

Meanwhile, cook noodles in rapid boiling water for three minutes then drain, rinse well in cold water and drain again.

Combine the soy sauce and mirin in a bowl.

Add the noodles to the vegetables and resume stir-frying. Sprinkle on the seeds and nuts. Make sure the vegetables and noodles are reheated. Just before you are ready to take it off the heat, drizzle on the soy and mirin, stir it through then serve while everything is hot.

Serves 4.

This is a lovely meal with the vegetables still on the crisp side of tender and the taste of the noodles shining through.

和

mushroom wellingtons

3 cups of mushrooms, finely chopped
1 large brown onion, finely chopped
2 cloves of garlic, crushed
1 tablespoon of olive oil
2 cups of fresh breadcrumbs
2 tablespoons of fresh parsley, chopped
1 tablespoon of thyme, chopped
2 teaspoons of fresh oregano, chopped
3 tablespoons of tamari
1 cup of brazil nuts, finely chopped
pinch of nutmeg
pinch of pepper
4 sheets of vegan friendly puffed pastry

Heat olive oil in a large heavy-based pan (such as a cast iron) then sauté the onion and garlic. Add the mushrooms and cook until soft. Now add the breadcrumbs, tamari, parsley, thyme, oregano, nuts, nutmeg and pepper. Gently stir and heat it all through (If you are using dried herbs, instead of fresh, halve the quantity, such as 1 teaspoon of dried oregano instead of two teaspoons of fresh.)

Allow the mixture to cool. Pre-heat the oven to 180 degrees. Cut pastry sheets into four square quarters. Now spoon mixture into each square and fold corners over to make individual parcels and pop them into the oven for 15 to 20 minutes.

Makes about 16 parcels.

These wellingtons have a great salty mushroom taste and need no added salt. They go well with fresh green salads in summer and the likes of crisp steamed vegetables in cooler months.

和

penne pasta and vegetables

500 grams of penne pasta
3 tablespoons of olive oil
3 zucchinis, sliced
2 cloves of garlic
3 spring onions, chopped
1 red capsicum, cut into strips
420 grams of sweet corn kernels
3 tomatoes, roughly chopped
2 tablespoons of fresh parsley, chopped

Bring four litres of water to the boil in a large pot. Add the pasta and cook for 15 minutes, until just tender. Drain, return to the pot and set aside.

Heat two tablespoons of the oil in a large frying pan. Add the zucchini and cook for three minutes, keeping stirred. Add the garlic, spring onion, capsicum and corn to the pan and stir-fry for three minutes. Stir the tomato into the mixture and cook for a further two minutes them set aside.

Add the parsley and remaining oil to the pasta and toss to combine. Place the pasta on plates and top with the vegetables and serve.

Serves 6 people.

A fresh tossed salad sets this dish off.

和

rice, peas and cashews

1 cup of basmati rice
½ a cup of peas
½ a cup of roasted cashews, roughly chopped
2 tablespoons of olive oil
pinch of turmeric
pinch of hing powder*
½ teaspoon of salt
1¾ cups of water
½ handful of coriander leaves

(* The herb hing, or asafoetida yellow, is a gum resin from the roots of Central Asian plants which is traditionally used in Indian cooking to add a garlic-like flavour.)

Rinse rice and place it in a medium sized saucepan with the olive oil and hing. Stir over a gentle heat for 30 seconds then add the water, peas, turmeric and salt.

Bring to the boil, cover and turn down to simmer for 18 minutes. Once cooked, stir in the cashews and serve with a garnish of coriander leaves.

Serves 4

This dish has a subtle taste which complements corn on the cob, home-made oven roasted potato chips and other lightly cooked vegetables. It brings a great yellow colour to a meal and also goes well with stronger tasting foods, such as samosas.

和

spaghetti bolognaise

2 medium onions, finely chopped
2 tablespoons of olive oil
7 medium mushrooms, finely chopped
2 stalks of celery, finely chopped
2 medium carrots, finely chopped
4 garlic cloves, crushed
800 gram tin of tomatoes, mashed
1 generous handful of fresh oregano, finely chopped
1 teaspoon of salt
1 teaspoon of ground black pepper
1 teaspoon of brown sugar
1 generous handful of fresh parsley, finely chopped
1 tablespoon of red wine vinegar
2 cups of fresh green beans, trimmed and cut into 5cm lengths
600 grams of spaghetti

Put oil in a large saucepan and warm over a medium heat. Add the onion and sauté for three minutes. Add the mushrooms, celery, carrot and garlic and sauté for three minutes. Stir in the oregano, salt, pepper, sugar and tomatoes with a little water and simmer for 20 minutes. Stir occasionally. Turn off the heat and mix in the parsley and red wine vinegar. Put lid on the saucepan and set it aside.

Bring four litres of water to the boil, add the spaghetti and gently stir for a moment to prevent it clumping. Bring water back to the boil and cook, with the saucepan lid off, for 10 to 12 minutes. Meanwhile, lightly cook the beans in boiling water, then drain.

Serve as soon as the spaghetti is ready. Spoon the sauce on and have the beans off to one side.

The sauce flavour is enhanced if you cook it in the morning, put a lid on the

和

saucepan and let it sit until you are ready to eat that evening. Simply warm the sauce as you cook the spaghetti and beans.

Serves 6.

This spaghetti bolognaise is a real crowd pleaser. It's a classic vegan meal that I've seen turn the head of many meat eaters.

和

spiced lentil and vegetable tagine

1 ½ cups of brown lentils
2 tomatoes, roughly chopped
600 grams of butternut pumpkin, peeled and cut into 3am cubes
3 medium sized carrots, peeled and cut into 2cm lengths
1 small sweet potato, peeled and cut into 2cm lengths
3 tablespoons of olive oil
1 onion, finely chopped
3 garlic cloves, finely chopped
½ teaspoon of ground cumin
½ teaspoon of ground turmeric
¼ teaspoon of ground cayenne pepper
1 teaspoon paprika
3 teaspoons of tomato paste
½ teaspoon of sugar
1 tablespoon of parsley
2 tablespoons of chopped coriander
1 teaspoon of sea salt
ground black pepper, to taste

Put lentils in a sieve and rinse in cold water. Remove any stones. Tip into saucepan and add one litre of water. Bring to the boil and skim the surface, if necessary. Cover and simmer over a low heat for 20 minutes.

Heat a large saucepan over a medium heat, add onion and cook until soft. Add garlic and cook a few seconds then stir in cumin, turmeric and cayenne. Cook for 30 seconds, then add paprika, tomato, sugar, sea salt, black pepper to taste and half the parsley and coriander.

Add undrained lentils and the prepared pumpkin, carrots and sweet potato. Stir well and simmer for 20 minutes or until vegetables and lentils are tender. Adjust seasoning. Sprinkle with remaining parsley

和

and coriander. Serve hot or warm with crusty bread.

Serves 4 to 6.

This dish is also beautiful when served on boiled rice with steamed beans, corn on the cob and broccoli. A twist of fresh lemon will enhance the flavours.

和

spicy corn fritters

2 cups of fresh corn kernels, (about 3 cobs)
2 cups of self-raising flour
1 ½ handfuls of parsley, finely chopped
1 fresh red chilli, very finely chopped
1 small purple onion, finely diced
½ a red capsicum, finely chopped
salt and freshly ground pepper to taste
about a cup of vegetable oil

Using a knife, trim the kernels from about three cobs of corn and set aside.

Put flour in a medium sized mixing bowl and keep adding enough water to make a runny but still thick batter. Use a balloon whisk to make a smooth batter.

Then, using a wooden spoon, mix in the corn kernels, parsley, chilli, onion, capsicum, salt and pepper. If you don't have a fresh chilli, use a ¼ teaspoon of chilli powder.

Heat a small amount of vegetable oil in a frypan and, using a tablespoon, spoon the batter mixture into roughly 6cm by 6cm fritters. Make them about 1cm thick. The mixture should not be too runny. Add a touch more flour if the fritters run too much when you spoon them into the pan. Add a little more water if the mix is too stiff.

Cook until golden brown on both sides and then lay them out on paper to soak out some of the oil once they're cooked. Lightly coat the pan with a little more oil before adding the next batch.

Makes about 30 fritters.

These simple little morsels are great at barbecues with a splash of homemade tomato sauce and a basic fresh garden salad of lettuce or bok choy, tomato, carrot and fresh green beans.

They keep well in the fridge to re-heat, eat cold or use on lunch sandwiches.

和

spicy thai tofu and noodle soup

400 gram block of firm tofu, rinsed and cut into about 2cm cubes
100 grams of snow peas, trimmed
1 head of broccoli, cut into small florets
1 handful of fresh coriander, finely chopped
3cm piece of fresh ginger, finely chopped
2 garlic cloves, finely chopped
1 teaspoon of grated lemon rind
1 medium chilli, finely chopped
1 litre of vegetable stock
440 millilitre can of coconut milk
½ a red capsicum, cut into strips
1 stalk of celery, finely chopped
1 medium onion, finely chopped
2 medium carrots, peeled and cut into julienne sticks
2 teaspoons of thai seasoning
1 tablespoon of vegetable oil
250 gram packet of fresh hokkien noodles

Heat oil in a large saucepan and add the onion, ginger and garlic and sauté, stirring frequently until the onion is translucent.

Add tofu, thai seasoning, lemon rind, chilli and coriander. Stir over a medium heat until tofu is well coated and flavours combined.

Place noodles in a heatproof bowl and cover with boiling water to soften and separate. Drain and set aside the noodles.

Add stock to the tofu mixture and bring to the boil. Add vegetables and simmer for one minute then add noodles and simmer for another minute. Reduce the heat to a simmer, add coconut milk and continue gently simmering until the vegetables are just cooked and serve immediately.

Serves 4.

和

super quick green asian stir-fry

1 tablespoon of sesame oil
3 garlic cloves, finely sliced
6 spring onions (or shallots), chopped
3 bunches of baby choy sum (or bok choy), washed and trimmed
1 bunch of broccolini
1 carrot, thinly sliced
½ red capsicum, thinly sliced
1 cup of cauliflower flowerettes

dressing
2 tablespoons of tamari
2 tablespoons of mirin
1 cup roasted cashews

Heat oil in a wok, stir-fry garlic 30 seconds. Add vegetables and stir-fry until cooked but still crisp.

Mix the tamari and mirin together.

Remove vegetables from the wok, drizzle dressing over them and add the cashews. Serve immediately.

Serves 4.

Having the vegetables crunchy in a slightly undercooked way is what makes this dish extremely appealing.

和

sweet potato and coconut dhal

550 grams of sweet potato, peeled and cut into 2cm cubes
175 grams of split red lentils, rinsed and drained
1 red chilli, finely chopped
400 millilitre can of coconut milk
450 millilitres of water
1 teaspoon of grated fresh ginger
½ teaspoon of ground cinnamon
½ teaspoon of turmeric
salt and pepper (to taste)
1 tablespoon of fresh coriander, chopped

As dhal is served with steamed rice, see page 152 for rice absorption cooking method.

Put sweet potato into a saucepan with lentils, chilli, coconut milk and water. Bring to the boil then reduce heat to simmer for 15 to 20 minutes, until the potato and lentils are tender and the mixture is thick.

Stir in the ginger, cinnamon, turmeric and some salt and pepper when the lentils are tender and cook gently for a few minutes.

Sprinkle the dish with chopped coriander as it is served with steamed rice.

Serves 4.

This is a mild dhal, so if you wanted to make it more firey, double the chilli. And to make it a complete meal you could steam some vegetables, such as cauliflower, broccoli, carrots, green beans or peas to go with it.

和

thai pumpkin curry

2 tablespoons of vegetable oil
½ bunch of shallots or 1 large onion, sliced
2 garlic cloves, crushed
1 teaspoon of freshly grated ginger
2 dessertspoons of thai red curry paste
750 grams of kent pumpkin, peeled, cut to about 3cm cubes
400 millilitres of coconut cream
150 millilitres of vegetable stock
zest of 1 lime, plus its juice
2 teaspoons of grated palm sugar
400 grams of fresh green beans, chopped into 3cm lengths
generous handful of coriander, finely chopped
½ cup of roughly chopped roasted peanuts
2 cups of basmati rice

Heat oil in a large pan, add shallots, garlic and ginger. Stir-fry for three to four minutes. Mix in the curry paste and pumpkin and stir-fry for another three to four minutes.

Add the coconut cream, stock, palm sugar, lime zest and juice. Bring to the boil, reduce heat and simmer gently until the pumpkin is just tender. Stir frequently to prevent sticking, but try not to mush up the softening pumpkin.

Add the beans, season with salt and pepper and cook for another three minutes.

While all this is going on, give the rice a quick rinse, place it in a saucepan with three cups of water, stir to distribute and put the lid on. Bring water to the boil, turn heat down and simmer for 10 minutes with the lid on.

Serve by spreading a bed of rice, spoon the curry on top and then sprinkle it with the coriander and nuts.

Serves 6.

This is a yummo meal that has lovely smooth flavours. And it goes nicely with mango and avocado salsa.

和

tofu and cashew curry

1 cup of coconut milk
1 heaped teaspoon of green curry paste
1 teaspoon of sea salt
½ large red onion, finely chopped
1 clove of garlic, crushed
⅓ cup of water
350 gram block of firm tofu, cut into 1cm-2cm cubes
1 cup of green beans, 2cm lengths
1½ cups of cauliflower flowerettes
⅓ cup of cashews, toasted
handful of coriander, roughly chopped
salt and freshly ground pepper, to taste

Place half the coconut milk in a saucepan and bring to a simmer over medium heat. Whisk in the curry paste and salt and remove lumps. Stir in the onion and garlic and cook for one minute.

Stir in the remaining coconut milk, water then tofu. Cook down the liquid for a couple of minutes before adding beans and cauliflower.

Cover and simmer for two minutes and remove from heat. Add cashews and adjust the salt and pepper to preferred taste.

Serve with fresh coriander sprinkled on top.

Serves 4.

This is a delightful 'creamy' dish that is wonderful with greens and steamed rice. It can also add complimentary interest to a plate with anything hot and spicy.

和

tofu in satay sauce

350 gram block of firm tofu
2 tablespoons of vegetable oil
1 fresh long chilli, or 3 small ones
1 medium brown onion
1 medium red capsicum
½ a cup of peanut butter
½ cup of coconut cream
¼ cup of sweet chilli sauce
2 tablespoons of soy sauce
½ cup of roasted, unsalted peanuts
2 cups of basmati rice

Cut tofu into blocks of about 1½ cm square. Heat the vegetable oil in a large pan, add the tofu cubes and cook over a medium heat until golden brown. Remove from pan and place on absorbent paper.

Cook the basmati rice. See page 152 for absorption method.

Meanwhile, cut onion into six then thinly slice it, take seeds out of chilli, slice it thinly and halve, core and thinly slice capsicum. Place these three ingredients, with a touch of vegetable oil, in the pan and stir-fry until soft.

Add a quarter cup of water along with the peanut butter, coconut cream, sweet chilli sauce, soy sauce and peanuts to the onion mixture and stir it all together. Now add the tofu and stir-fry it all until hot. You may want to add a little more water to make the sauce less concentrated and ensure the tofu is well covered.

Serve by laying a bed of rice on the plates and place tofu and satay on top.

Serves 4.

This dish is great by itself and can be a fantastic crowd pleaser when served with steamed or lightly boiled green vegetables such as broccoli, beans or peas.

和

tomato and basil soup

1.5 kilos of ripe tomatoes, cut in half
2 garlic cloves
1 teaspoon of olive oil
1 tablespoon of balsamic vinegar
1 tablespoon of dark brown sugar
1 tablespoon of tomato puree
300 millilitres of vegetable stock
2 tablespoons of chopped fresh basil
salt and pepper, to taste

Preheat oven to 200 degrees. Evenly spread the tomatoes and unpeeled garlic on an oven tray or roasting pan.

Mix oil and vinegar together. Drizzle over tomatoes and garlic then sprinkle with sugar. Roast for 20 minutes, until tender and slightly charred.

Remove from the oven and cool slightly. Squeeze out garlic and blend (or sieve) tomatoes and garlic pulp to a smooth consistency.

Add to this the tomato puree and vegetable stock. Place in a pan and heat gently, stirring occasionally and season with salt and pepper to taste before serving.

Serves 4.

和

tofu laksa

400 grams of firm tofu, cut into about 1.5 cm cubes
1½ tablespoons of vegetable oil
500 millilitres of water
200 grams of rice noodles
375 millilitres of vegetable stock
400 millilitres can of coconut milk
250 grams of bean sprouts
⅓ cup of chopped fresh coriander leaves
4 green shallots, sliced thinly
extra coriander leaves to garnish

curry paste
 1 medium brown onion, chopped
 2 garlic cloves, crushed
 3cm piece of fresh ginger, peeled and grated
 1 teaspoon of grated lemon rind
 ½ cup brazil nuts (or macadamia nuts)
 1 teaspoon of sesame oil
 1 tablespoon of soy sauce
 1 tablespoon of sambal oelek (a chilli paste)
 1 tablespoon of fresh lemon juice
 1 teaspoon of ground cumin
 1 teaspoon of ground coriander

Make the curry paste by placing all the paste ingredients into a food processor and process until they're well combined, then set it aside.

Make the vegetable stock by placing two teaspoons of vegetable stock powder in one and a half cups of hot water.

Cook the noodles in a large saucepan of boiling water for two minutes, drain and set aside.

和

Heat vegetable oil in a large saucepan over a medium heat and cook the tofu. Turn it occasionally until it's lightly golden. Remove it from the pan and set aside.

Add the vegetable stock and curry paste to the saucepan and bring it to the boil. Reduce heat to low, stir in the coconut milk and fried tofu and simmer gently for three to five minutes.

Be careful to simmer the soup gently as the coconut milk may separate if boiled.

Stir in the chopped coriander.

To serve, rinse noodles in hot water to reheat. Drain and divide them into four deep serving bowls. Ladle in the soup, top it with bean sprouts and garnish with green shallots and coriander leaves.

Serves 6.

和

vegetable pullao

2 cups of basmati rice
3 tablespoons of olive oil
1 teaspoon of yellow mustard seeds
1 teaspoon of wholemeal mustard
1 hot green chilli, finely chopped
1 ½ cups of potato, peeled and cut into 1cm dice
1 ½ cups of carrot, peeled and cut into 1cm dice
1 ½ cups of fresh green beans, cut into 1cm lengths
1 ½ tablespoons of sesame oil
½ teaspoon of ground turmeric
1 teaspoon of garam masala
1 teaspoon of very finely grated fresh root ginger
1 ¼ teaspoons of salt
1 cup of roasted cashews

Wash rice several times then leave it soaking in water for about half an hour or so.

Put oil in a large heavy pan on medium to high heat. When hot, pop in the mustard seeds for 20 seconds, then put in the potato, carrot, beans, mustard, chilli, turmeric, garam masala, salt and ginger.

Stir together, sauté for about a minute then reduce heat to medium-low. Drain rice, add it to the other ingredients, stir it in and cook for two minutes. Add 800 mililitres of water and bring it to the boil. Put the pan lid on, reduce heat to very low and cook for 25 minutes.

Sprinkle with cashews as you serve in individual bowls.

Serves 6.

This subtle tasting dish is great by itself, laid over some green leaves or with lightly steamed broccoli.

和

watermelon curry

¼ large watermelon
1½ teaspoons of chilli powder
¼ teaspoon of ground turmeric
½ teaspoon of ground coriander
1 clove of garlic, crushed
salt to taste
2 tablespoons of vegetable oil
½ teaspoon of cumin seeds
3 teaspoons of lime juice

Cut melon into 3cm cubes and remove seeds. Take one cup of melon and blend to make juice. Add chilli, turmeric and coriander to juice along with garlic and salt. Heat oil in a wok, add cumin seeds and roast for 30 seconds. Add melon juice mixture, lower heat and simmer for five minutes so that spices cook and liquid reduces by one third. Add a pinch of sugar and lime juice and cook for one minute.

Now add the melon pieces and cook over a low heat for three to four minutes, turning gently until all pieces are covered in spicy mixture.

Serve as a side dish.

Serves 4.

This is a tasty surprise that adds another dimension to our traditional summertime treat, watermelon.

和

vegie and chickpea tagine

400 gram tin of cooked chickpeas
1 kilogram of pumpkin, peeled and
cut into 2.5cm cubes
½ a cauliflower, broken into flowerettes
400 gram tin of chopped tomatoes
2 cups of vegetable stock
175 grams of thin green beans, topped and
chopped into 2 cm lengths
2 tablespoons of chopped mint
2 tablespoons of chopped fresh coriander
1 lemon, cut into 6 wedges
2 tablespoons of olive oil
1 onion, chopped
2 garlic cloves, crushed
1 tablespoon of grated ginger
2 teaspoons of ground cumin
2 teaspoons of ground coriander
1 teaspoon of paprika
1 cinnamon quill
2 cups of rice
extra sprigs of mint or coriander for garnish
salt and pepper, to taste

Heat the oil in a large deep saucepan over a medium heat. Add the onion and cook for four minutes or until softened. Add garlic and ginger and cook for 30 seconds, stirring until fragrant.

Add cumin, ground coriander, paprika and cinnamon quill then stir for one minute. Add the pumpkin, tomatoes and stock and stir to combine. Season with salt and pepper. Bring to the boil then reduce

和

heat to simmer for 15 minutes uncovered or until pumpkin is tender.

Add cauliflower and beans and cook for a further five minutes or until they are just tender.

In a separate saucepan, cook rice using the absorption method (see page 152) as the tagine is simmering.

Just before serving, add the mint and fresh coriander to the tagine. As the cinnamon quill was used just to flavour the dish it can now be discarded.

Serve the tagine and rice with a wedge of lemon and garnish with a sprig of mint or coriander

Serves 6.

Great for a casual meal with family and friends by the fire. Instead of chickpeas you could vary this tagine by adding a handful of whole nuts, such as almonds, walnuts or cashews just before serving.

和

vegie burgers

1 good sized sweet potato
½ cup of vegetable oil
1 onion, finely chopped
2 garlic cloves, crushed
½ a teaspoon of ground cumin
1 cup of raw cashews, roughly chopped
400 gram tin of cannellini (or butter) beans
1 tablespoon of tahini paste
juice of two lemons
fresh multigrain bread, about five slices
salt and pepper to taste
dessertspoon of sweet chilli sauce
1½ handfuls of fresh parsley, finely chopped
¾ cup of plain flour

Peel the sweet potato, cut it into 1cm cubes and place it in a saucepan with just enough water to cover it. Cook until tender but not too soft, about 15 minutes. Then drain, set aside and let cool.

Heat a small amount of vegetable oil in a large pan and add the onion and garlic. Cook until soft, add the cumin and cook for a further 30 seconds to combine, then take off the heat. This pan can be used later to cook all the burgers.

Using a food processor (kitchen whiz), process the breadcrumbs down until they are fairly even, without big lumps. You should have at least two cups of breadcrumbs. Set them aside in a large mixing bowl.

Drain and rinse the cannellini beans in water.

Using the processor, process the beans with the onion mixture, cashews, tahini and lemon juice. Put it all in together before you start the machine, rather than adding ingredients.

和

Whiz it all for about 30 seconds to chop the cashews up a bit, but not too small, as you want to retain pieces for texture rather than having it too smooth.

Now, add this mix to the breadcrumbs in the bowl along with the sweet potato, salt and pepper, chilli sauce and parsley. Stir it all with a fork until it is an even mix. You may need a little more lemon juice to help hold it together if it is too dry.

It is best, but not essential, if the sweet potato is cool when forming the patties.

Put plain flour in a shallow dish or bowl then, using a tablespoon, form each patty and coat them in flour. Heat a small amount of oil in your large pan and fry the burgers.

Makes about 30 burgers.

These treats taste terrific and are very versatile. They're a real hit at barbecues with a splash of homemade tomato sauce. They go with all sorts of salads and vegetable dishes, tomato, peanut or white sauces. You name it. As long as there are no inquisitive teenagers in the house, they can last in the fridge to provide a week or so of leftover meals and sandwich lunches. Or, you can throw them in the freezer until needed. They're lifesavers.

和

vegie samosas

1 large onion, finely diced
3 cloves of garlic, crushed
2 ½ cm long piece of root ginger, peeled and grated
1 kilogram of kent pumpkin, diced to about 2cm
3 large potatoes, diced to about 2cm
3 large carrots, diced to about 2cm
1 stick of celery, diced to about 2cm
2 cups of frozen peas
1 teaspoon of curry powder
½ teaspoon of chilli powder
generous handful of parsley, finely chopped
1 sprig of fresh mint, finely chopped
1 teaspoon of vegetable stock
juice of 1 lemon
2 tablespoons of vegetable oil
10 vegan friendly puffed pastry sheets

Using a large boiler, heat the oil and sauté the onion until soft. Add garlic and ginger and sauté for another minute, stirring so they do not burn.

Add all the diced vegetables and vegetable stock with enough water to not quite cover the lot. Without the lid on, bring to the boil, reduce heat and simmer until the vegies are tender. You want to boil off a lot of the liquid. Watch it and stir frequently. You want a thick vegetable mixture that is mushy but able to be spooned out rather than runny and watery. You could start with less water and add a little more as you're cooking or if it ends up too runny just pop the finished vegies in a colander and drain off the excess liquid.

When the vegetables look close to being cooked add the lemon juice, peas, parsley, mint, salt and pepper to taste and set aside to cool.

和

It is best if vegetables are cooked either the morning before their intended teatime use or the night before as this not only allows them to cool but enhances the flavours.

Preheat oven to 200 degrees.

Thaw out 10 puffed pastry sheets and cut each into four squares.

Place a tablespoon of vegetable mixture into the centre of one square, fold the diagonal corners together then pinch the sides in so you have a triangle of pastry filled with vegetable mixture.

Do this with all your pastry and place the triangles about 2cm or so apart on either non-stick or oiled baking trays and bake for about 15 to 20 minutes, or until puffed and golden.

You could spray the samosas with a little water and sprinkle sesame seeds on top before baking.

Makes about 40 samosas.

These samosas are spicy and go well with cool, fresh salads and subtle tasting dishes such as rice, peas and cashews. They freeze well.

和

zucchini muffins

1 tablespoon of vegetable oil
4 medium zucchini, grated
1 medium onion, finely chopped
2 garlic cloves, peeled and crushed
2 cups of self-raising flour
1 teaspoon of chilli paste (like sambal oeleck)
¾ cup of soy milk
an extra ¼ cup of vegetable oil
1 teaspoon of salt
½ teaspoon of ground pepper
¼ cup of sesame seeds

Preheat oven to 160 degrees.

Heat one tablespoon of oil in a medium saucepan and sauté onion and garlic until soft. Grate zucchinis into a bowl and stir in the soy milk, extra oil, salt, pepper and chilli paste.

Add sauted garlic and onion to this mixture and mix well. Then add self-raising flour and mix well again.

Spoon mixture into oiled muffin tins or patty papers in muffin tins, sprinkle with sesame seeds and bake for about 20 minutes, or until cooked.

You can make this zucchini mix into a slice, if that's preferred. If so, grease and line a 22cm by 28cm slice tin, spread the mixture out and cook in a 160 degree oven for 30 to 40 minutes, or until cooked.

Makes about 12 muffins.

These muffins are delicious straight out of the oven, and they freeze well. They have a dense texture (which I love) rather than being light and fluffy. They're an ideal savoury bite when out on your bike for several hours.

和

salads, sauces and such

asparagus (blanched)

1 bunch of asparagus

Cut a centimetre or so off the bottom of the stalks (as this piece can be a bit woody when bought from a shop) then cut the stalks in half so they are 10 centimetres or so long.

Put enough water in a saucepan to just cover the bunch and bring it to the boil. Now pop the asparagus in the water, bring it back to the boil and leave the asparagus there for about 30 seconds. Turn off the heat, drain the water and eat the asparagus as soon as possible.

As a light bite by itself, I find a plate of asparagus an absolute treat. Usually though it's eaten with a meal so, in that case, leave its cooking right to last so it's warm with the rest of the dish.

It's great if you grow your own, but if you buy it from a shop, eat it as soon as you can to maximise the freshness. Asparagus dries out from the bottom, so the longer you leave it in the fridge the more woodiness you should cut off the stem's base.

和

balsamic and garlic dressing

2 tablespoons of balsamic vinegar
¼ cup of lemon juice
1 garlic clove, crushed
¾ cup of olive oil

Put all ingredients in a lidded jar and shake well. This dressing can quickly transform a garden salad.

和

beetroot, couscous and sweet potato salad

300 grams of orange sweet potato, chopped
3 tablespoons of olive oil
½ teaspoon of sea salt and cracked pepper
850 gram can of baby beets, drained and halved
2 cups of couscous
½ cup of chopped chives
½ cup of flat leaf parsley, chopped
¼ cup of basil leaves, chopped or left whole
1 tablespoon of lemon zest

Preheat oven to 200. Combine sweet potato, 1 tablespoon of olive oil, salt and pepper in bowl, toss to coat.

Place on a baking tray and cook for 20 to 30 minutes or until cooked through and slightly browned. Allow to cool.

While sweet potato is cooking, put couscous into the serving bowl with the lemon zest and pour in two cups of boiling water. Stir lightly with a fork and cover bowl with a large plate or tray to keep steam in.

Assemble just prior to serving and lightly combine all ingredients in the serving bowl with the couscous and remaining oil, salt and pepper to taste.

Serves 4.

If you don't have the oven on for anything else, to justify the power use, you could pan fry the sweet potato. Use garlic chives from the garden and extra basil if no parsley. It still tastes great.

和

cardamom marinade for tofu

grated rind and juice of 1 lemon
4 green cardamom pods
1 tablespoon of balsamic vinegar
1 tablespoon of olive oil

Crush the cardamom pods with a mortar and pestle and remove the husks. Then combine all ingredients in a jar and shake. Pour the mixture over a block of tofu which has been cut or cubed ready for cooking and placed in a bowl. Let it sit as long as possible so the tofu can soak in the flavours. Leave it overnight if you can, one hour at least. When ready to cook the tofu, take it out of the marinade and lightly pan fry it in a little oil.

和

char-grilled capsicum, bread and tomato salad

2 red capsicum, seeded and chopped roughly
10 chat potatoes, washed, unpeeled, cut in half
3 cups of bread chunks, about 2cm (sourdough or Turkish)
6 roma tomatoes, quartered lengthways
1 red onion, thinly sliced
2 cups of fresh basil or baby spinach leaves (or a combination of both)
¼ cup of olive oil

dressing
⅓ cup of red wine vinegar
¼ cup of olive oil
1 tablespoon of raw sugar
1 garlic clove, crushed
1 tablespoon of capers, rinsed, drained and very finely chopped
salt and pepper, to taste

Make dressing by combining all ingredients in a lidded jar and shaking well. Set it aside.

Place chats in boiling water in a large saucepan and cook until just tender. Drain and set them aside.

Preheat oven to 180 degrees.

Drizzle some olive oil over a large oven tray, lay out bread chunks and drizzle them with a bit more of the oil and bake until they're crisp and golden.

Repeat this process with the chats and set them aside to cool slightly.

Heat a heavy frypan, add a splash of olive oil and the capsicum. Char the capsicum over a high heat while stirring frequently. Remove from pan and set them aside to cool slightly.

In a large serving bowl, combine the tomatoes, basil, onion and capsicum.

Just before serving, add the toasted bread and roasted chats. Drizzle them with the shaken dressing and toss lightly before immediately serving.

Serves 6.

和

chinese noodle salad

½ chinese cabbage
½ bunch of shallots, finely sliced

dressing

1 tablespoon of soy sauce
1 tablespoon of brown sugar
¼ cup of white vinegar
½ cup of olive oil
½ teaspoon of sesame oil
½ cup of slivered almonds, toasted
½ cup of sunflower seeds, toasted
100 grams of plain fried noodles

Trim off any coarse pieces of the cabbage and then slice the remainder finely. Place the finely sliced shallots in a large serving bowl with the cabbage and mix well.

Dressing:

Put the soy sauce, sugar, vinegar and oils in a lidded jar and shake well. Just before you're ready to serve, pour the dressing onto the cabbage and shallots and add the almonds, seeds and noodles. If fewer than six people are to share the salad only mix the appropriate proportion together. By keeping the remaining ingredients separate and combining them when needed, say the next day, everything stays crisper.

Serves 6.

和

coriander marinade for tofu

grated rind and juice of 1 lemon
2 spring onions, finely chopped
2 garlic cloves, crushed
2 tablespoons fresh coriander, chopped
1 red chilli, remove seeds, finely chop

Combine all ingredients in a jar and shake. Pour it over a block of tofu which has been cut or cubed ready for cooking and placed in a bowl. Let it sit for at least an hour. Leave it overnight if you can, the longer the better to allow flavours to soak into the tofu. When cooking the tofu, take it out of the marinade.

和

creamy mushroom sauce

1 tablespoon of vegetable oil
1 small onion, finely chopped
250 grams of mushrooms, cleaned and sliced
1 shallot, finely chopped
1 cup of white sauce (see recipe, page 246)

Heat oil in a frypan and sauté onion until soft. Add mushrooms and cook until limp and slightly brown. Stir often to prevent burning. Add shallot and the white sauce, which in our household is often a leftover from a meal earlier in the week. It will last several days in the fridge and can be frozen.

Stir to mix well and heat through, adjusting the seasoning to taste. Add extra water to make the sauce more runny. Serve hot with cooked pasta.

Serves 2 with rice.

This sauce is also great on vegetables and offers a surprising change from tomato sauce on vegie burgers.

和

fennel, orange and almond salad

2 baby fennel bulbs (or 1 large one)
2 cups of fresh orange juice
2 large oranges, skinned and cut into segments
100 grams of baby spinach leaves
½ cup of flaked almonds

Bring juice to the boil and reduce to two tablespoons. Cool.

Set aside fennel tips and thinly slice bulb.

Place fennel in a serving bowl with spinach leaves and orange segments. Toss gently.

Drizzle with cooked reduced orange juice and sprinkle with almonds. Garnish with pieces of the green fennel tips and serve.

Serves 4.

和

fried noodle salad

200 grams of asian fried noodles
100 grams of asian salad greens
1 cup of bean sprouts
¼ purple cabbage, finely shredded
½ a bunch of shallots, chop into 5mm pieces
½ a red capsicum, finely chopped
¼ cup of coriander, finely chopped
1 carrot, cut in thin long strips
100 grams of roasted cashews

Mix all these ingredients together in a large bowl.

dressing

¼ cup of seasoned rice vinegar
1 tablespoon of soy sauce
½ cup of olive oil
¼ cup of castor sugar
2 teaspoons of sesame oil

Whisk the dressing in a separate bowl or make it in a lidded jar which you can shake to mix. Pour over the salad items just before eating.

Serves 4

和

gado gado

2 potatoes, cut into 2cm cubes
4 carrots, cut into matchsticks
100 grams of snow peas, finely sliced
200 grams of cauliflower, cut into flowerettes
1 lebanese cucumber, sliced into coins
½ a medium lettuce
1½ cups of alfalfa sprouts
½ a bunch of shallots, cut into 1cm ringlets
½ a cup of fresh coriander, coarsely chopped

dressing

½ cup of roasted peanuts, roughly chopped
2 garlic cloves, crushed
3 purple onions, coarsely chopped
½ teaspoon of sugar
1 tablespoon of soy sauce
½ teaspoon of chilli powder
1 tablespoon of lemon juice
¾ cup of water
140 millilitre can of coconut milk

In boiling water cook the potatoes and cauliflower until they are just tender. Drain, and keep the cooking water to use to cook the carrots and peas until just tender. Allow them all to cool before placing them in a large serving bowl with the cucumber, sprouts, lettuce, shallots and coriander.

Dressing: Using a mortar and pestle (or stick blender) grind the nuts, garlic and onions into a rough paste and cook in a lightly oiled pan for two minutes. Add the sugar, soy, chilli powder, lemon juice, water and coconut, bring to the boil then simmer for three minutes.

Drizzle the dressing over the potato mixture when ready to serve.

Serves 4.

和

garden salad

¼ lettuce
2 tomatoes
½ purple onion
2 carrots

Bunch the lettuce together and slice it every centimetre or two and pop it into a serving bowl. Cut the tomatoes in half then each half into quarters and put them in the bowl. Slice the onion fairly finely and throw it in. Purple onions look interesting and have a milder taste than some other onions. If you prefer a more onion tasting salad use a whole one, or stronger tasting one and don't cut it too small. Wash the carrots and slice them in half, top to toe, and then through the middle. Now carefully cut them lengthways so they're like big matchsticks. Put them in, mix everything and serve.

Serves 2.

We all start somewhere. Yes this is simple, but it goes together in a jiffy and is rarely out of place. If you have a bit more time, or want something more elaborate, throw in other ingredients such as chopped beetroot, capsicum, cashews, almonds or other nuts, a little sliced pineapple or avocado.

和

green bean and french lentil salad

⅔ *cup of french-style green/black lentils*
500 grams of baby green beans, trimmed
2 medium tomatoes, chopped
¼ *cup of finely chopped fresh chives*

vinaigrette dressing
1 shallot, finely chopped
1 tablespoon of dijon mustard
2 tablespoons of red wine vinegar
2 tablespoons of olive oil

Cook lentils, uncovered in boiling water for about 15 minutes, until tender than drain.

Make vinaigrette by whisking the shallot, mustard and vinegar together then whisking in the oil to thicken. You could substitute a finely sliced purple onion for the shallot. Cook beans until just tender and drain.

Place beans, tomatoes, lentils and chives into a serving bowl and toss with dressing.

Serves 6.

This nice salad is even better warm. If you're organising a big family meal, try it alongside the warm potato, pear and pecan salad (see page 245).

和

hummus

300 grams of tinned chickpeas
juice of 1 lemon
2 garlic cloves, crushed
salt to taste
2 generous dessertspoons of tahini paste

Using blender or food processor, blend drained chickpeas with lemon juice then add remaining ingredients. If mixture is too thick just add small amounts of extra water or lemon juice as desired.

A splash of sweet chilli sauce is a nice addition with some finely chopped coriander.

Makes enough for 6 people.

Leftovers keep for a week or so in the fridge and also freezes well.

和

julie's tomato sauce

5 kilograms of tomatoes, chopped roughly
1.2 litres of brown vinegar
2 tablespoons of coarse salt
3 cups of white sugar
½ a knob of fresh garlic
1 teaspoon of ground cloves
1 teaspoon of allspice (pimento), ground
1 teaspoon of ground peppercorns
Pinch of cayenne pepper

Place all ingredients in a large boiler. Bring to the boil and then over a low to medium heat gently boil to half the original volume. This will take three to four hours. Keep an eye on it. Stir occasionally to prevent burning on the bottom. Blend the mixture in a blender or food processor until smooth. Use clean, recycled glass bottles that have been rinsed in hot water just before filling with sauce. Seal bottles while sauce is hot.

Makes 3 litres.

Yes, I know it takes a fair bit of time and the cooking process will fill the house with a vinegarish smell, but it's worth it. This sauce will spoil you. I reckon you can splash it on almost anything. I know that's a bloke sort of thing to say, but it's right. At any barbecue vegos and meat-eaters alike will knock you over to get at it. It settles in the bottle over time, but just give it a shake and away you go again.

和

lemon, lime and rice salad

2 cups of basmati rice
½ a cup of almonds, roughly chopped
¼ cup of pumpkin seeds (pepitas)
¼ cup of sunflower seeds
½ cup of fresh coriander, thinly sliced
½ cup of fresh parsley, finely chopped

dressing

¼ cup of olive oil
¼ cup of lemon juice
1 teaspoon of lime zest
3 tablespoons of lime juice
¼ teaspoon of black pepper

Cook two cups of rice (see page 152) and set it aside in a big serving bowl. Once cool add the remaining salad ingredients and mix gently.

Place all the dressing ingredients in a lidded jar, shake well and drizzle over the salad just before serving.

和

mango and avocado salsa

1 ripe mango, peeled and deseeded
1 ripe avocado, peeled and deseeded
1 small red onion, finely chopped
juice of one lime
1 small bird's eye chilli, very finely chopped
salt to taste

Cut the mango and avocado into about 1cm pieces then combine all ingredients gently, but thoroughly in a bowl. Add salt, and a little extra lime if desired, to taste.

Makes a nice dip or accompaniment for a tagine or curry for four and it adds a nice touch to a piece of toast.

和

mick's pumpkin and coriander dip

3 cups of cooked butternut or kent pumpkin
3 tablespoons of olive oil
4 tablespoons of peanuts, crushed
3 tablespoons of sweet chilli sauce
4 tablespoons of lemon juice
1 teaspoon of cumin
2 garlic cloves, crushed
1 tablespoon of fresh ginger, chopped
(or ½ teaspoon of ground ginger)
1 tablespoon of fresh coriander, chopped roughly

Put all the ingredients in a blender or food processor and blend well together.

This dip is great with raw vegies, such as carrots and celery, on cracker biscuits or as a sauce over rice or cooked vegetables.

和

nachos

2 tablespoons of vegetable oil
3 x 400 gram tin of kidney beans
2 x 400 gram tin of tomatoes
1 medium onion, finely chopped
3 cloves of garlic, crushed
1 generous teaspoon of vegetable stock powder
½ teaspoon of chilli flakes or chilli powder
salt and pepper (to taste)
1 avocado
1 lemon
1 lettuce
2 packets of 200 gram corn chips

Heat oil in a large saucepan and add onion, garlic and chilli powder. Sauté until onion is translucent. Drain and rinse kidney beans in a colander then add them to the onion mixture.

Roughly chop the tomatoes and add them to everything in the saucepan. Using a potato masher, mash the beans and tomatoes well to make a sauce. Add salt and pepper to taste and bring the saucepan mixture to the boil.

Spread a bed of shredded lettuce on your plates and cover the lettuce with corn chips. Put your nachos mixture all over the chips and top it with mashed avocado seasoned with salt, pepper and lemon juice to taste.

Serves 6 to 8.

Nachos are easy to put together, tasty and if they could talk it would probably be in Spanish. The bean sauce mixture can be made in large quantities, popped into the deep freeze and brought out when needed. It's great with salad, on wraps, toast or as a taco filling. Tinned kidney beans are quicker, but if you like you can buy dried kidney beans, soak them and cook according to packet recommendations.

和

oven roasted tomato and garlic sauce

2 kilograms of ripe tomatoes
2 large onions, roughly chopped
12 garlic cloves, unpeeled
4 tablespoons of olive oil
2 tablespoons of balsamic vinegar
1 tablespoon of sugar
½ a teaspoon of salt
½ a teaspoon of freshly ground black pepper

Heat oven to 200 degrees. Cut tomatoes in half and spread them out (so they can cook more evenly) with the onions and garlic on a large oiled oven tray. Drizzle olive oil over tomatoes, onion and garlic to lightly coat them.

Bake for one hour or until tomatoes are soft and slightly scorched and onions are cooked.

Remove from oven and cool for 15 minutes. Pick out garlic cloves, carefully squeeze the soft mushy garlic out of their skins, discard skins and put garlic and tomatoes into a food processor with balsamic vinegar, sugar, salt and pepper.

Process it all to your desired consistency – smooth or chunky.

Makes about 3 cupfuls.

This is a great sauce with pasta.

和

pesto

2 handfuls of fresh basil leaves
1 handful of raw cashews
juice of 1 lemon
1 garlic clove, crushed
¼ cup of extra virgin olive oil

Rinse the basil leaves and, while damp, put them in a jar or container, roughly 10cm in diameter and at least that tall. Put all the other ingredients in also and, using a stick blender, blend everything until it is smoothish. (A stick blender, for people like me who have never heard of one until now, is a long, skinny device with blades at the bottom not something made of sticks.) If this recipe is too stiff for your liking, add a bit of water or more lemon juice.

Makes about a cup full.

This pesto is yum, having really great flavour if you've just picked the basil leaves from your own garden. It can be used as a dip, sauce or spread. If you have an abundance of basil in your garden during summer make several batches of pesto as it freezes and revives well. Pesto really picks up a salad or can be drizzled over finely sliced or shredded raw zucchini to great effect.

和

quinoa (pronounced keen–whah) orange and pumpkin salad

1 cup of red quinoa, rinsed
1 tablespoon of extra virgin olive oil
2 brown onions, diced
1½ tablespoons of red wine vinegar
2 tablespoons of orange juice
1 teaspoon of orange zest
300 grams of pumpkin, peeled and grated
½ cup of pumpkin seeds (pepitas)
2 tablespoons of fresh mint leaves, finely chopped
pinch of black pepper
pinch of sea salt

Place the quinoa in a saucepan with one and a half cups of water and a pinch of sea salt and bring to the boil. Reduce heat, cover and simmer for 12 minutes or until water is absorbed. Set aside in a large bowl to cool.

Heat a small amount of vegetable oil in a saucepan and sauté the onion for about six minutes or until transparent. Add the vinegar, pepper and orange juice and simmer for two minutes. Add the pumpkin and heat through. Remove from the heat and allow to cool slightly.

Add the pumpkin mixture to the quinoa with the pumpkin seeds, mint and orange zest and mix well.

Serves 6.

This salad is both an eye catcher and a taste sensation. It can be served warm, cool or as a leftover from the fridge for several days.

和

real guacamole

2 ripe avocados
juice of 1 lemon
2 ripe tomatoes, skinned
2 garlic cloves, crushed
½ red onion, very finely chopped
sea salt to taste
½ small fresh red chilli, remove seeds

Roughly mash the avocados and lemon juice into a bowl. Remove seeds and juice from the tomatoes and finely chop. Add the tomatoes, garlic, onion, salt and chilli to the avocado and mix well.

Serves 4.

Guacamole is a nice cracker dip or topping to go with nachos.

和

red capsicum and cashew nut dip

2 red capsicum, deseeded and roughly chopped
3 garlic cloves, crushed
juice of ½ a lemon
1 small bird's eye chilli, deseeded and finely chopped
½ a purple onion, finely chopped
1 tablespoon of parsley, finely chopped
1 cup of raw cashews
salt, to taste

Using a food processor, chop up the cashews to a fairly fine consistency, but not a paste. Remove from the processor and set aside in a bowl.

Into the processor put all the remaining ingredients and process to a fairly even consistency.

Add this to the cashews and adjust to taste with salt and lemon juice.

Makes enough dip for about 6 people.

和

satay sauce

1 tablespoon of vegetable oil
1 onion, finely chopped
2 garlic cloves, crushed
½ teaspoon of chilli powder
1 teaspoon of curry powder
2cm of fresh ginger, finely chopped
125 grams of roasted peanuts, chopped
½ cup of brown vinegar
¼ cup of sugar
1 teaspoon of salt
2 tablespoons of peanut butter
⅓ cup of fruit chutney
1 cup of water
1 heaped teaspoon of vegetable stock powder

Heat the vegetable oil in a medium saucepan, add the chopped onion and crushed garlic. Saute gently until golden brown.

Add the chilli powder, curry, fresh ginger and chopped roasted peanuts, vinegar, sugar, salt, peanut butter, fruit chutney, water and vegetable stock. (A vegetable stock cube could substitute for the vegetable powder, if you prefer while a quarter teaspoon of powdered ginger could replace fresh ginger and red wine vinegar replace brown vinegar if that's in your pantry.) Mix the ingredients well and simmer very slowly for about 20 minutes. Keep the mix stirred as it thickens so it doesn't catch on the bottom and burn.

Serves 6 with rice.

If you like a fairly firey satay sauce add more chilli powder and it will greatly liven up rice dishes and all sorts of vegetables.

和

spiced nuts

500 grams of mixed raw nuts
2 tablespoons of olive oil
1 dessertspoon of sea salt
1 teaspoon of sugar
2 teaspoons of sweet paprika
½ teaspoon of cayenne pepper
fresh rosemary sprigs for garnish

Preheat oven to 180 degrees. In a bowl, combine nuts, oil, salt, sugar and spices – coat nuts well. Spread out on a large oven tray and bake in a moderate oven for 10 minutes, until fragrant and toasted.

Cool on paper towel then transfer to a serving bowl and garnish with rosemary sprig tips.

和

sunday night salad

2 medium orange sweet potatoes, peeled and diced into about 2cm chunks
1 teaspoon of good quality curry powder
½ teaspoon of salt
1 tablespoon of vegetable oil
2 handfuls of baby spinach leaves
2 medium tomatoes, cut into about 2cm pieces
3 medium zucchini, sliced
1 cup of tinned chickpeas, drained and rinsed
1 tablespoon of fresh parsley, finely chopped
1 lime

Preheat oven to 180 degrees. Put sweet potato chunks into a bowl and coat with oil and sprinkle with curry powder and salt. Toss until well coated then spread out on a greased oven tray or baking dish and bake until tender. It should take about half an hour, just keep an eye on it.

While potato is cooking, place spinach leaves, tomatoes and chickpeas into a serving bowl.

Then put half a cup of water in a small saucepan, bring it to the boil, add sliced zucchini, simmer until they're just cooked and drain straight away. You want the zucchini to still be a little crisp.

When sweet potato is cooked add it and zucchini to ingredients in the bowl, sprinkle on parsley, squeeze lime juice on top, toss to combine it all and serve immediately.

Serves 4.

The warm sweet potato stands out, particularly as the curry gives it a fragrant spiciness.

和

warm choko salad

4 chokos
2 firm tomatoes
1 small red onion
1 small chilli, finely chopped
dressing
½ teaspoon of dijon mustard
6 tablespoons of red wine vinegar
4 tablespoons of olive oil
salt and pepper to taste

Slice chokos in half then peel and core. Place them in a saucepan of water and cook until just tender then drain. Quench in cold water, drain and set aside to cool.

Make dressing by combining all ingredients in a lidded jar and shake.

Cut chokos into wedges, about four slices from each of the cooked halves. Combine them with the tomatoes, onion and chilli in a serving bowl, pour the dressing over the top and serve.

Serves 4.

This salad is delicious by itself or as an accompaniment to another dish, say, tofu in satay sauce for an even more interesting meal.

和

warm potato, pear and pecan salad

900 grams of chat potatoes, unpeeled
1 teaspoon of dijon mustard
2 teaspoons of red wine vinegar
3 tablespoons of olive oil
2 teaspoons of poppy seeds
2 firm, ripe dessert pears
2 teaspoons of lemon juice
175 grams of baby spinach leaves
75 grams of toasted pecan nuts
salt and pepper, to taste

Cook potatoes in lightly salted water for 15 minutes until tender. Drain, cut into quarters and place in a serving bowl.

Make the dressing in a small bowl by whisking together the mustard and vinegar. Gradually add the oil until the mixture thickens. Stir in the seeds and season with salt and pepper.

Pour two thirds of the dressing over the hot potatoes and toss gently to coat. Leave until potatoes have soaked up the dressing and are just warm.

Meanwhile, quarter and core the pears. Cut into thin slices then sprinkle with lemon juice to prevent them from going brown. Add to potatoes with spinach leaves and pecans. Gently mix together and drizzle the remaining dressing over the salad and serve.

Serves 6.

This lovely tasting salad has more texture than some.

和

white sauce

2 tablespoons of vegetable oil
2 tablespoons of plain flour
salt and freshly ground pepper
1 teaspoon of wholegrain mustard
3 cups of soy milk
1 tablespoon of chopped parsley

Place the vegetable oil in a medium saucepan and heat over a medium heat. Add the plain flour to the warm oil, combine well and continue stirring over the heat for one to two minutes. You have to cook the oil and flour mixture without burning it so be careful the mixture does not brown.

Remove saucepan from the heat and gradually add the soy milk. Initially, stir constantly with a wooden spoon to remove lumps as the mixture thickens. Using a wire whisk helps remove lumps as the mixture thickens.

Return the mixture to a medium heat and stir frequently until the sauce comes to the boil and fully thickens. Add seasoning to taste plus the mustard and parsley and keep stirring until it boils.

If it is too thick for your desired use, add more soy milk.

Serves 4 with rice.

This sauce is delicious on cooked vegetables, vegie burgers, nutty rice and noodles. It is a great stand-by to keep in the freezer and whip out on short notice.

和

sweets

alison's banana cake

450 grams of ripe bananas, mashed
50 grams of chopped walnuts
100 millilitres of cold-pressed sunflower oil
100 grams of raisins
75 grams of rolled oats
150 grams of whole wheat flour
1 teaspoon of vanilla essence
a pinch of sea salt

Preheat oven to 190 degrees. Mix all the ingredients together. The consistency should be soft and moist. Brush the base and sides of a 500 gram loaf tin with oil then spoon in the cake mixture. Bake for 50 minutes or until a skewer comes out of the cake clean. Cool for 15 minutes before turning out.

Serves 8.

Afternoon tea with the ladies anyone?

和

apple fritters

2 cups self-raising flour
4 medium green apples
a few teaspoons of vegetable oil

Gradually add water to the flour and stir it into a thick but runny batter. Peel, core and thinly slice the apples and add them to the batter, making sure they are well covered.

Put a light film of oil in a frypan and heat it. Using a tablespoon as a rough measure, spoon your mixture into the hot pan, patting each fritter down to about 1cm high. When they bubble on top a little they're ready to flip to cook the other side. After taking the first few out, add some more oil before the next ones go in. If time allows, place them on paper as you take them from the pan to soak up the oil.

Serves 4.

These fritters are quick and easy. They are great hot with soy ice cream and a leftover treat during the next few days, if they ever last that long.

和

carrot muffins

4 medium carrots, grated
1 cup of walnuts, chopped
1 cup of sultanas
2 cups of self-raising flour
1 teaspoon of baking powder
1¼ cups of soy milk
1 teaspoon of mixed spice
¾ a cup of sugar
¾ cup of vegetable oil

Preheat oven to 160 degrees. Oil muffin tins or line with muffin papers.

In a mixing bowl, combine sugar, oil, milk, sifted flour, baking powder and mixed spice and beat well by hand.

Add carrot, walnuts and sultanas and stir well. Then spoon the mix into prepared muffin tins.

Now cook for about 25 minutes, or until golden.

Makes about 20.

These morsels are simple and very more-ish.

和

christmas pudding

250 grams of sultanas
250 grams of currants
250 grams of raisins
½ cup of vegetable oil
2 cups of fresh breadcrumbs
1 granny smith apple, peeled, grated
1 cup of plain flour
1 teaspoon of ground ginger
1 teaspoon of mixed spice
1 teaspoon of nutmeg
½ teaspoon of salt
1 teaspoon of bicarbonate of soda (bicarb)
round calico pudding cloth, about 60cm diameter
50cm long piece of strong string

Put pudding cloth in a large boiler filled with water and bring to the boil. Keep it simmering as you want the cloth hot and the water boiling to cook the pudding. Put on a kettle of water also to ensure you have enough boiling water to cover the pudding right from the start. It's good to have hot water on hand to quickly bring to the boil when needed to top up water the pudding is in. Don't top up with cold water as you want the pudding sitting in a gentle, rolling boil from start to finish.

Now, put the sultanas, raisins and currants in a bowl with the oil and mix. Stir in the breadcrumbs and grated apple. Next, mix in the flour and spices with half a cup of cold water.

Mix it all together, adjusting the water if necessary, so the result is a moist mixture that is stiff enough to stand up a wooden spoon.

(Traditional puddings also had a few surprise sixpences. Ours still does,

和

but they're not a good idea if people eating the pudding don't know they're in it or the pudding is to be eaten by unsuspecting children.)

Remove the cloth from the boiling water, squeeze it and lay it on the bench top. Rub plain flour into the cloth to about 75mm from the edge.

Tip the mixture into the cloth, gather up the edge in a pleating motion all the way round and tie it off with the string as close to the pudding as possible. Tie a loop in the string so you can slip a broom handle through it when the pudding is cooked.

Put a kitchen plate in the boiling water in the boiler and then put in the pudding. The plate keeps the pudding off the boiler's bottom and rattles about throughout the cooking process so you know the water is still boiling.

Boil the pudding on a gentle boil for five hours.

Keep an eye on the water level and top it as required.

When the time is up, remove pudding from water, loop the string over a broom handle and hang the pudding suspended from the broom handle between two chairs to let it cool. Using clothes pegs, peg the cloth's top to keep it off the pudding.

After half an hour cooling, put the pudding on a bench and carefully take off the cloth.

Whacko!

Let it properly cool before cutting.

For reuse, soak the cloth in cold water and then scrub it roughly with a brush to get the bulk of residue pudding mix off. Now soak it in warm soapy water, brush it again and soak it in fresh water before a final brushing and hanging it on the clothesline to dry.

和

coconut rice with rhubarb and strawberries

1 cup of wholegrain rice
200 millilitres of coconut cream
¼ cup of sugar
½ bunch of rhubarb, leaves discarded
½ punnet of strawberries
1 tablespoon of chopped almonds or toasted sesame seeds

Combine rice and water in a saucepan, bring to the boil with the lid on and immediately reduce heat to a simmer. Still with the lid on, simmer for half an hour, turn the heat off and allow the rice to steam with the lid on for 10 minutes. Then add the coconut cream and half the sugar, mix well and set aside.

Trim and chop the rhubarb into 2cm lengths. Put it in a medium saucepan with one tablespoon of water and remaining sugar. Bring to the boil and simmer until soft, stirring occasionally. While rhubarb is cooking, slice the strawberries into a bowl and once the rhubarb is cooked pour it onto the strawberries.

To serve, spoon some rice into a dessert bowl, cover it with rhubarb and strawberries and top with almonds or sesame seeds.

Serves 4 to 6.

This dish is sweet so a spoonful or two of soy ice cream or a cool, chopped banana can be complimentary.

和

date scones

1 ½ cups of dried dates
1 dessertspoon of icing sugar
3 cups of self-raising flour
1 teaspoon of baking powder
¼ cup of vegetable oil
1 cup of soy milk
½ cup of plain flour, for kneading

Pre-heat oven to 160 degrees.

Roughly chop dates and put them in a saucepan with one third of a cup of water. Stir and bring them to the boil. Put the lid on and simmer for a few minutes so they absorb the water. Turn off the heat and set the dates aside to cool. Add the oil and half the soy milk to the dates.

Using vegetable oil, lightly oil a baking tray. Place greaseproof paper on the bottom of the tray and lightly oil it also. A tray about 22cm wide and 28cm long should hold about 20 scones in total.

In a big bowl, sieve or mix well the self-raising flour, icing sugar and baking powder. Make a hollow in the centre of the dry ingredients and pour in the dates, oil and soy milk. Using a wooden spoon, combine it all together adding the rest of the soy milk gradually as you go. Stir until you have a slightly sticky soft dough mixture. You need a consistent mixture, not too dry, not too sloppy so some days you may need a little more milk, some days less.

Sprinkle some plain flour on the bench top. Lightly knead the mixture into the flour so it is coated and press it down to about 3cm thick. Don't overdo it with the kneading as you don't want the mixture to be too stiff.

Dip a round scone cutter into what is left of the half cup of plain flour and begin cutting into your mixture. Continue to dip the cutter in flour between scones to stop it sticking. Fill the tray so that each scone

和

date scones (continued)

is touching the one next to it. Put the tray in the oven on a 15 minute timer. Keep an eye on them as sometimes they will need a little less and sometimes a little more oven time.

They're just right when the top is lightly brown and they sound hollow when tapped with your fingernail. Get them out of the tray by placing a tea towel over a cake cooler, turn it upside down and put it over the scones. Now turn the lot over and the scones should slide out into the tea towel.

Makes about 20.

Eat scones straight out of the oven. They are fantastic with a splash of jam and a blob of soy ice cream. If they're not eaten immediately wrap them in the tea towel to hold the moisture in and, once cool, put them in an air-tight container.

和

family gramma pie

pastry

> *1 quantity of sweet short crust pastry (see page 262)*

filling

> *2.5 kilogram piece of gramma*
> *1 cup of sultanas*
> *2 tablespoons of sugar*
> *1 teaspoon of mixed spice*
> *juice of 2 lemons*

Peel and remove seeds from the gramma then chop it into 3cm chunks. Place the pieces in a large saucepan, just cover with water, put lid on and bring to the boil. Simmer until cooked then drain and mash well. Add sultanas, sugar, mixed spice and lemon juice. Mix in well and set aside.

Divide the pastry in half and roll each into a circle with about a 30cm diameter. Place both pastry rounds onto prepared oven trays. Put half the filling on each piece of pastry and spread it to about 4cm from the edge. Fold up the pastry edges all the way around leaving some filling exposed in the middle. You should now have two pies with about 20 cm diameters. Place them in the preheated oven and cook for 20 minutes, or until golden.

Another alternative is gramma crumble.

You make the gramma filling as suggested above.

For the crumble you'll need

> *1 ½ cups of plain flour*
> *2 tablespoons of brown sugar*
> *½ cup of sunflower seeds*
> *1 cup of nuts (brazil, almond or hazel will do)*
> *1 teaspoon of ground cinnamon*
> *⅓ cup of vegetable oil*

和

family gramma pie/crumble (continued)

Pre-heat the oven to 160 degrees.

Mix the flour and sugar well in a large bowl with a fork. Chop the nuts fairly small so they will be distributed in every mouthful of the crumble. Mix them in along with the seeds and cinnamon. Drizzle in the oil and combine everything evenly with a wooden spoon. The oil will make the mixture clump together so keep going until it is all a fairly even consistency.

Pre-heat the oven to 160 degrees. Put the gramma in one or two oven-proof dishes and spread the crumble about 1cm thick on top.

Bake the crumbles in the oven for 15 to 20 minutes so the top is golden brown and the gramma is heated through.

Makes 2 pies with a total of least 8 hearty servings.

Gramma pies and gramma crumbles are a fantastic blast from the past. Soy ice cream really sets them off.

和

rhubarb crumble

See the family gramma pie recipe (previous page) for details on how to make the crumble mixture

rhubarb filling

1 bunch of rhubarb

3 green apples

½ teaspoon of grated nutmeg

1 tablespoon of raw sugar

Remove rhubarb leaves, trim the heel ends and cut into 2cm lengths. Peel and thickly slice the apples into about four slices per quarter.

Put the rhubarb and apple into a large saucepan with half a cup of water. Bring to the boil and then turn the heat down with the lid on to simmer for five or six minutes until the rhubarb is soft. Stir occasionally to prevent sticking. Once cooked add sugar and nutmeg to taste.

Serves 6 (with crumble).

和

sanwin makin (burmese semolina slice)

4 cups of coconut milk
1⅓ cups of semolina
1 cup of sugar
¾ cup of sultanas
2 tablespoons of poppy seeds
tablespoon of vegetable oil

Preheat oven to 130 degrees. Grease a 28cm by 22cm baking dish with vegetable oil and line it with baking paper.

Combine the semolina, sugar and coconut milk in a large saucepan. Let it stand for half an hour then put it over a low heat until it comes to the boil, stirring frequently as it thickens. The mixture should be thick but not stiff.

Add sultanas, mix them in well then pour it all into the prepared baking dish. Smooth the top of the mixture and sprinkle it evenly with poppy seeds.

Bake in the oven until golden on the edges and set in the middle. It will take about 45 minutes, but keep an eye on it so it doesn't burn. Allow to cool, refrigerate overnight, then slice to serve

Makes a tray full that can be cut into 20 or so nice size pieces.

和

simple fruit cake

1 kilogram of mixed dried fruit
440 gram tin of crushed pineapple
½ cup of vegetable oil
1 teaspoon of bicarbonate of soda (bicarb)
1 cup of self-raising flour
1 cup of plain flour

Place in a large saucepan the dried fruit, pineapple and the natural juice in the tin, plus the vegetable oil. Bring to the boil and simmer for two minutes, keeping it stirred so the fruit soaks up as much liquid as possible. Put the lid on and set it aside to cool. It's good to allow it to sit overnight. Or, you could do this step in the morning and continue the cake in the evening.

The second step begins by pre-heating the oven to 150 degrees.

Sieve the self-raising and plain flour into the fruit mix and combine well. You want a wet but stiff mixture. If it is a bit dry add a little water.

Using vegetable oil, oil a 22cm diameter round cake tin. Place greaseproof paper on the bottom of the tin and oil it lightly. Pour in the mixture and press it down with a fork to about 2cm from the top.

Place tin in the oven and put the timer on for 50 minutes. After that time test the cake by poking a wooden skewer into the middle of it. If it comes out clean it is cooked. If the skewer has cake mix on it put the cake back in the oven for five minutes and test it again.

Makes one 22cm diameter round cake.

This is very sweet cake. For a more crunchy texture try adding a handful or so of chopped brazil nuts to the fruit mix.

和

sweet short crust pastry

1 cup of self-raising flour
1 cup of plain flour
¼ cup of sugar
¼ cup of canola oil
cold water

Place all the dry ingredients into a food processor bowl and process for a few seconds as you drizzle in the oil and then add just enough cold water to form a dough ball that comes away from the sides of the bowl.

Stop processing immediately or you will make your dough tough.

Set dough aside in a covered bowl to rest for 20 to 30 minutes while you prepare your filling (apple, gramma, for instance) and while the oven preheats to 160 degrees.

Lightly knead dough on floured bench top then roll to desired thickness and size. Assemble your pie, or slice, and bake at 160 degrees until golden.

Makes enough for two medium sized pies.

和

dedication

I owe so much to:
Parents, Mary and Frank Maguire,
who had difficult clay to mould.
Wife, Julie, a devil's advocate who,
for reasons best known to her, has
cared, loved and still endures.
(Without Julie this book would not exist.)
Our five children,
Bonn, Grace, William, Eve and Hope
who always light the way.
Plus commoners, ninja, unseen forebears,
those whom I have not seen eye to eye,
wild animals and
the most humble of trees.

Thank you.

defining approach

A vegan is a person who tries to live each day in practical harmony with all life. Vegans apply a commonsense approach to eating plant-based food created from vegetables, fruit, nuts, seeds, legumes and pulses, such as beans, peas and lentils. They apply commonsense to not eating meat or using animal products. This includes all types of flesh plus eggs, butter, cheese, honey, leather, wool, silk, fur and consumer commodities containing animal ingredients and products tested on animals. Vegans encourage diversity and attempt to serve through advocacy, education and non-violent action. They aim to improve themselves and the wider world through integrity of thought and efforts to reduce exploitation, injustice, abuse, pollution and waste. Also, they strive to learn from their mistakes and continual human failings through conscious consideration based on love and a generous spirit. In essence, the path of a selfless heart beats strong through a trusting flexibility that recognises life is about living, rather than remaining confined within convention or idealism.

koori recognition

I wish to acknowledge the Koori people,
the indigenous men, women and children
who inhabited Australia at the time of
white people's occupation.

You bore the brunt of that settlement from
1788. We owe you a debt of gratitude for
having nurtured the earth and, after initial
uprisings, choosing a peaceful and productive
path in the face of on-going brutality
and injustice.

Hopefully all people may come to appreciate
your salutary legacy and the importance of
country.

I have used the word Koori in this book as an alternative to the English word Aboriginal.

I do so as a mark of respect for all Australia's indigenous people, noting that the word Koori comes from languages of eastern coastal Australia and is more common in this area where I also live. I accept that it is not the word approved by all indigenous people but understand it to be favoured by many from my region as more appropriate today than the old English word.

spicks and specks

Avocado is a subtle tasting fruit rich in fatty acids, nutrients, protein and fibre. It's great in salads and a natural alternative to butter as a spread on bread.

A bunch of kale will stay noticeably fresh and crisp if you put it in a container of water in the fridge. It only needs about five centimetres in the bottom of the container.

A calorie is the energy needed to raise the temperature of one gram of water one degree celsius at sea level.

A chest freezer is usually much more energy efficient than an upright.

Add a little soy sauce to tone down sugar in sweet things.

All oven temperatures in this book are degrees of celsius

A pinch, a touch and a smidgin are just small quantities.

Cook tops and ovens need cleaning (this is a skill I've had difficulty mastering to Julie standards).

Chickpeas: While it's handy to have a few tins in the cupboard, they taste better, are cheaper and more environmentally friendly if you buy dry ones and cook them yourself, following packet directions.

Clean and dry knives as you use them. Some food left on blades can tarnish even stainless steel.

Julienne is a way to prepare vegetables and fruit as a garnish by cutting them into thin strips about the length and thickness of matchsticks.

Keep an eye out for supermarket specials, such as soy milk, then buy several cartons and freeze until needed.

Kumara is orange sweet potato.

Leafy green vegetables of all kinds stay fresher and crisper if they're kept in an air-tight container in a fridge. They'll keep many days longer by comparison with leaving them in a fridge crisper.

Lentils are little seeds that grow in pods (like the common pea) on small bushes. They aid vitality, healthy skin, growth and our sight.

One kilogram (kg) equals 2.2 pounds (lb).

Quinoa (pronounced keen-whah) is a seed with more protein than any other grain. It is high in B vitamins and iron, a great source of calcium and contains all the essential amino acids our bodies can't make on their own.

Saute means to pan-fry food in a very small amount of oil.

Season to taste, or add seasoning, simply means to add salt, pepper, herbs, spices, fruit juices and other condiments to suit your individual liking.

Tahini paste is made from ground sesame seeds and is also called sesame paste.

The most power efficient fridge and freezer you can afford are worth paying a little extra for. Lower electricity bills will probably cover the initial higher purchase price in a few years.

To convert one cup of plain flour to self-raising, add two teaspoons of baking powder

Wash chopping boards as they are used. Food is harder to remove when dry and can discolour wood and bamboo.

Zest is the grated layer of skin from citrus fruit, usually lime, lemon or orange.

resources

Substantially, this book hovers on recycled information and opinion.

It is far from being a humanist, nutritional or ecological tome.

Even so, I would like it taken a little seriously.

Therefore, to add a touch of gravitas, here is a list of references from which I have drawn.

To avoid it reaching biblical proportions I have not quoted every chapter or verse.

books, reports and articles.

Animal Dreaming by Scott Alexander King; Australian Bureau of Meteorology's 2009 Annual Climate Statement; Australian Bureau of Statistics various reports; Australian Collaborative Land Use and Management Practices, land use summary Australia 2009; Australian Federal Government's Climate Change Department's Climate Change Risks to Australia's Coast report, November, 2009; *Being Vegan* by Joanne Stepaniak; *Biological Science* third edition by Scott Freeman; *But You Kill Ants* by John Waddell; Culture Jam by Kalle Lasn; *Deforestation and Land Degradation in Queensland* by Gerard Bisshop and Lefki Pavlidis of Melbourne University; Department of Agriculture, Fisheries and Forestry meat, wool and dairy report 2009; *Food Additives* by Sue Treffers; Food Standards Australia various reports; GetUp organic farming legal battle press release Jan 2011; Green for Life by Victoria Boutenko; Greenpeace International various reports; *Hard to Swallow, a brief history of food* by Richard W. Lacey;

Journal of Alzheimers Disease (Vol 17, No 2, 2009); *Journey in Time* by George Chaloupka; *Koori: A Will to Win* by James Miller; *Macquarie Dictionary* fourth edition; *Measuring and addressing the ecological impact of household food waste in Australia* by David Baker of The Australia Institute; Melbourne University Water Use Study 2004; my life experiences; *Newcastle Herald* newspaper various reports; New South Wales Meat Industry Authority various reports; *Ninja: The Invisible Assassins* by Andrew Adams; Radio National's *The Spirit of Things* program; *Richard's Bicycle Book* by Richard Ballantine; *Sustainable Energy–Without the Hot Air* by David J.C. MacKay; *Sydney Morning Herald* various reports; *The Freedom Paradox* by Clive Hamilton; *The Gruen Transfer* by Jon Casimir; *The Independent on Sunday* various reports; *The Man Who Planted Trees* by Jean Giono; *The New Additive Code Breaker* by Maurice Hanssen, Jill Marsden and Betty Norris; *The Truth About Trees* by Julia Mitchell; The World Bank various reports; United Nations Food and Agriculture 2006 report *Livestock's Long Shadow; Vegan Nutrition: Pure and Simple* by Michael Klaper MD; Vegetarian Network Victoria various reports; Vegetarian Vegan Society of Queensland various reports; *Vitamin B12 supplementation: natural or unnatural*, compiled by Manuj Chandra; voiceless.org.au internet website; Wikipedia internet site various reports.

websites

The following cyber-signposts may help in a search for purposeful information.

This eclectic bunch drew my attention as *vegan ninja* was pieced together.

It is the tip of an iceberg.

animalsasia.org–Asiatic black bears, known as moon bears, are rescued by this group from an existence in tiny cages on 'farms' across China and Vietnam where they are being milked for bile that is used in traditional medicines.

animalsaustralia.org–This national animal protection organisation investigates and exposes animal cruelty, researches animal use alternatives and lobbies government representatives to improve protection laws.

asca.org.au–Advocates for Survivors of Child Abuse is an Australian national organisation to improve the lives of adult survivors of child abuse and neglect. Help is offered to access services for health, well-being and meaningful community engagement.

bikesforhumanity.com.au–This is a grassroots group that ships donated bicycles to Africa to help improve access to health care, education and employment. It is linked to other global organisations working with locals in Africa on training and other networking.

caritas.org.au–Poverty, peace and justice in Africa, Asia, Latin America and the Pacific are this aid organisation's focus. Its programs include education in Australian indigenous communities, confronting domestic violence in East Timor, tackling AIDS-related problems in El Salvador and sustainable food security in Malawi.

earthgarden.com.au/foundation–This is a body that works with the Himalayan Light Foundation to install donated solar power systems in Nepal. Solar replaces expensive, polluting kerosene lights in places such as schools, community buildings and health centres.

erc.org.au–The Edmund Rice Centre is involved in research, community education, advocacy and networking in fields, such as justice, poverty and inequality in Australia and overseas.

erc.org.au/pcp–Pacific Calling Partnership is a group of non-government organisations, individuals and community bodies seeking help for low-lying Pacific Island and Torres Strait islands threatened by climate change driven rising sea levels.

ewg.org–The Environmental Working Group is a non-profit organisation which aims to protect people from health risks associated with toxic contamination, such as agricultural pesticides, and improve public policy to protect the environment.

fta.org.au–Fairtrade is a social movement to help people in developing countries move towards stability and economic sustainability. It supports better produce prices, working conditions, wages and terms of trade.

humanecharities.org.au–This organisation lists health-related charities which do not fund or engage in animal testing. It aims to help discover safer medicines and abolish animal experimentation by increasing awareness of humane charities.

lovelifehope.com–Mission Mexico provides care and an opportunity to attend school for an average of 45 children who come from impoverished and abusive backgrounds. The refuge relies on donations and volunteer help to continue.

mawa-trust.org.au–Medical Advances Without Animals Trust is an Australian medical research and educational charity which concentrates on implementing solutions to advancing medical science and improving human health without using animals.

nepcam.org.au–This volunteer organisation reduces poverty for poor families in Nepal and Cambodia through education, child sponsorship and sustainable community projects. Its work includes grants to secondary students seeking higher education, teacher development courses and micro-business support.

orangutan.org.au–The Australian Orangutan Project focuses on saving orangutans in Sumatra and Borneo. These apes face extinction mainly because their rainforest habitats are being felled for palm oil and other crops.

pedalfest.org.au–Dungog Pedalfest is an annual September celebration of cycling and socialising in Australia's Hunter Valley which raises money for charity. In addition to an assortment of on-road and off-road riding, the weekend includes music, dance, food, and an art show.

roomtoread.org–This organisation improves childhood educational opportunities with the aim to break the poverty cycle in developing countries including Bangladesh, Cambodia, India, Laos, Sri Lanka and Zambia.

seedsavers.net–This network preserves open-pollinated seeds and the genetic diversity of plant varieties through education, seed exchange and research.

thebigissue.org.au–The Big Issue organisation helps homeless, disadvantaged and marginalised people and publishes a magazine that provides money for those who sell it on the streets and disadvantaged women who work as dispatch assistants.

thegreyman.org–This registered charity rescues children from trafficking and exploitation in South East Asian countries. Its members also help with education, family assistance, justice and community infrastructure.

thetradingcircle.com.au–Established by The Good Shepherd Sisters, this scheme works with women in Africa, Asia and Latin America. The women are paid a fair price for work to trade themselves out of poverty.

truefood.org.au–This Greenpeace site rates food and beverage companies according to policies and actions in Australia to exclude ingredients from genetically engineered (GE) products, including oils derived from GE crops.

vegansocietynsw.com and vegsoc.org.au–For all things vegan in New South Wales and Queensland. These sites include recipes, books, events, socialising, restaurants, products and other web links.

recipe index

www.ingramcontent.com/pod-product-compliance
Lightning Source LLC
Chambersburg PA
CBHW062037090426
42740CB00016B/2935